Crack Competitive Exams in Pharmacy (Drug Inspector, GPAT) In 21 Days

Volume - I

Harshal Liladhar Tare

M.Pharm. (Pharmacognosy)

M.B.A. (HR and Marketing)

<u>**GPAT & NIPER PREPARATION PLAN**</u>

When you start preparation of GPAT and NIPER. First of all give importance to the GPAT, because the preparation strategy is different for GPAT and NIPER. Whereas GPAT concentrate on subject knowledge deeply and it is somewhat time taking to answer the questions when compare to the NIPER in which concentrate only on basics of subject especially in organic and stereo chemistry and analytical chemistry. And also when you qualified in GPAT then only you will be eligible for NIPER.

First divide all subjects from *simple to difficulty and according to their weightage in entrance exam.* According to my opinion I will give an idea First start with order

1. **Pharmacognosy**
2. **Pharmacology**
3. **Analysis**
4. **Pharmaceutical calculations**
5. **Pharmaceutical Jurisprudence**
6. **Biochemistry, Microbiology, Biotechnology**
7. **Pharmaceutics- physical pharmacy**
8. **Unit operations Bio pharmaceutics**
9. **Dispensing and clinical pharmacy**
10. **Medicinal Chemistry**

   (If u can study comparatively with pharmacology otherwise give last preference. Follow this order I think it is easy for you.)

➢ When you start preparation with pharmacognosy. First you should be concentrate on lecturing of lecturer. It helps to remember easy and can't easily forget.

➢ Prepare class running notes by simultaneous listening and note the important points and differences and note down the doubts separately and ask later class finishing to your lecturer.

➢ After Class College time it is better to revise on class notes and note the bits which are asked in previous exams.

➤ Before class starting once you check and observe the notes of yesterday.

➤ For every subject these steps are must be do then there is no tough feel in your preparation. Otherwise somewhat difficult you feel.

<u>Important topics for GPAT must study topics from each core subject for GPAT</u>

As we all know that the standard of GPAT exam has been increased many folds from last few years. So, now t requires lot of hard work and determination to go past through the hurdle of GPAT. The best thing about GPAT is that as now from this year total number of qualified students has been reduced to around three thousand only so the qualified students will get surely get admissions in the most premier pharmaceutical institutions of the nation.

So, if you are also a GPAT aspirant then don't be disheartened with the decreased number seats, instead work with double zeal to qualify GPAT with flying colors. The most important thing to require about the GPAT is that along with hard work one must also clear about the topics to be covered for GPAT preparation. In this article I am discussing the 5 most important topics of each core subject which must be studied for the GPAT preparation by every aspirant. So, now let us have a glance on each important topic one by one starting from the Pharmaceutics.

<u>IMPORTANT TOPICS OF PHARMACEUTICS FOR GPAT</u>

Pharmaceutics is the indispensable subject for those who wish to qualify GPAT with flying colors. Although one should study whole pharmaceutics thoroughly but if I am asked to give the most important topics, then I will recommend below 5 topics. Let me explain each topic one by one and explain.

(A) Tablet formulation-

Formulation of a tablet is the very first thing that a GPAT aspirant should start with the pharmaceutics. There are questions from this topic every year in the GPAT exam. In the formulation, one should study about different components used in the tablet formulation. One should also ponder on the different interactions among the different components of a tablet.

(B) Sterilization-

Sterilization is another topic for the GPAT. Every year I clearly 2-3 questions in the GPAT exam from sterilization. One should study thoroughly different technique of sterilization along with their mechanism. Microbial organisms used for the assay of sterilization are also important from the GPAT point of view.

(C) Numerical

Numerical is the area where most of the pharma students lack. But trust me this is the only area which can provide you edge over the other students. There are around 5-8 questions every year in the GPAT which tests the numerical ability of the student. Questions are generally asked from biopharmaceutics, dilutions, freezing point etc.

(D) Suspension & Emulsion formulation-

Formulation of suspensions and emulsions also do play an important role in the GPAT preparation. Due weightage is given to the surfactants and HLB scale in the GPAT exam. One should also study the evaluation of suspension and emulsions in detail.

(E) Rheology-

Rheology is also very scoring portion for the preparation of GPAT. In rheology, one should study types of flow with examples, different types of mills, angle of repose, Carr's index,

Important topics of Pharmacognosy for GPAT

Those who prepare for the GPAT know the importance of studying pharmacognosy to qualify GPAT. Pharmacognosy can be a deciding factor between the qualified and non-qualified students. Pharmacognosy is considered as the life line for the GPAT aspirants as it is the most scoring subject in the GPAT. Important topics for the GPAT include:

In each paper of GPAT irrespective of the year, I always find a question or two on the phytochemical screening. So, if studying two or three pages of phytochemical screening can earn you more than 5 marks in the GPAT then I don't think that it's a deal of loss. Phytochemical screening is best given in the CK Kokate's book pharmacognosy.

(B) Analytical Pharmacognosy-

Analytical Pharmacognosy is the other topic which holds high weight age in the GPAT exam. One should different stomata's, trichomes, moisture content, WHO guidelines in the analytical pharmacognosy. For this topic also CK Kokate is the best for GPAT purpose.

(C) General Pharmacognosy-

You must be wondering or confused that what should be studied by the students in general pharmacognosy? Let me explain it; in general pharmacognosy one should study thoroughly about general description, classification etc. of glycosides, alkaloids, terpenoids etc. In other words, one should study general pharmacognosy of glycosides, alkaloids and terpenoids.

(D) Biological source of all drugs-

Yes! You have read it right that for GPAT you have to learn the biological source of all the drugs along with their families. You will definitely find question on the biological sources in the GPAT exam. To avoid last minute confusion, I highly recommend that one should learn 10 new biological sources of drugs daily and revise the previous ones.

(E) Detailed study of selected drugs-

From the papers of last ten years, I have come to know that there are certain fixed drugs which have very high probability of asking in the GPAT exam. There are nearly about 30 such potent drugs with the point of view of GPAT. I will give details about them in my next article. Till then you can start your preparation with the detailed study of Digitalis, Senna and Atropa.

IMPORTANT TOPICS OF PHARMACOLOGY FOR GPAT

Receptors

This topic covers minimum 1-2 questions of the GPAT question paper every year. Students preparing for the GPAT must study different types of receptors along with their mechanism of actions. Questions on the receptors seem tricky in the GPAT exam but if this chapter is studied thoroughly then I am sure one can easily solve these questions. Beside from the GPAT, this is also a very interesting and knowledge worthy topic to read for a student of pharmacology.

Autonomic nervous system

Autonomic nervous system or ANS is of prime importance while studying for the GPAT. Every year ANS has 2-3 questions in the question paper of GPAT. In ANS, beta-blockers should be given utmost weightage while preparing the topic for GPAT. Different effect of sympathetic and parasympathetic nervous system should also be studied carefully while preparing for the GPAT exam.

Cardiovascular system

Next most important topic for the GPAT is cardiovascular system. This is also a very broad topic including cardiac agents, antihypertensive drugs, antiarrhythmic drugs and anti-lipidemic drugs. All these topics are of equal importance but cardiac glycosides can be given little extra importance. These drugs should be studied for their mechanism of action, drug interactions, side effects and main uses.

Anti-epileptic drugs

Epilepsy is also an important topic with respect to GPAT. The best book to study epilepsy and drugs used to treat is KD Tripathi Essential of pharmacology. In the anti-epilepsy along with mechanism and side effect of each class of anti-epileptic drug one must study the specific drug used to treat specific type of seizure.

Drugs used to treat cancer-

Cancer is also a hot topic with the point of GPAT exam. Classification of anti-cancer drugs along with mechanism of action should be thoroughly studied as every year there is a question on the anti-cancer drugs. Along with this, we should also focus his studies on the newer agents used for the treatment of cancer.

IMPORTANT TOPICS OF PHARMACEUTICAL CHEMISTRY FOR GPAT

From last few years trend has been made that questions asked in the GPAT has been shifted from the medicinal chemistry to core organic chemistry. There are quite good number of questions from the pharmaceutical chemistry portion of the syllabus. The questions asked in the pharmaceutical chemistry are very basic and test the knowledge of the student. Important questions of pharmaceutical chemistry include:

(A) Important name reactions-

Now from last few years, more number of direct questions has been asked from the name reactions. If one can observe then he will find that there hardly 20 important name reactions to study. If one can study these name reactions with mechanisms then definitely he will be able to solve 2-3 questions in the GPAT. Important name reactions for GPAT include: Aldol condensation, Cannizaro reaction, SN1 and SN2 reactions, Rimer-tieman reaction etc.

(B) Basic reaction mechanism

Next important topic to cover for the GPAT in pharmaceutical chemistry is basic reaction mechanisms. One should thoroughly study electrophilic and nucleophilic substitution and addition reactions. Whole organic chemistry revolves around these four basic types of reaction mechanisms. So, if one can command over these four reaction mechanisms then he can answer many questions of organic chemistry.

(C) Basics of organic chemistry

Beside from name reactions and reaction mechanisms, there are still lots of things to be considered in the organic chemistry. These basics include reaction intermediates (Carbocation, Carboanion, Free radical and Carbene), Aromaticity, catalysts in organic chemistry, Acidity and basicity of organic compounds, polarity etc. These topics often contain questions in the GPAT exam hence must be studied deeply.

(D) SAR studies of important drug classes

Structural activity relationship is an integral part of the medicinal chemistry. Most of the time examiner do ask question from this section to check the knowledge of the student. Important classes of drugs whose SAR studies are of due importance for the GPAT include Antipsychotics, Diuretics, Benzodiazepines, Acetyl Choline etc.

(E) Spectroscopy

The last but one of the most favourite topics of the examiner is the GPAT. If you are preparing for GPAT then you can't neglect the importance of this section. Every year there are definite questions either on number of signals of NMR, solvents used in different techniques, basic principles of spectroscopy etc.

OTHER MISCELLANEOUS TOPICS FOR THE GPAT

Beside from these core subjects, there are certain other topics which should also be studied while preparing for the GPAT. These topics include

a) All schedules of the drugs (Drug and cosmetic act)

b) Vaccine

c) Constitution of AICTE and PCI.

d) Biogenetic precursors of different classes of drugs.

e) Uses of microorganisms

f) Chemotherapy

So, these were the topics which in my analysis are the hottest topics for the GPAT preparation.

PHARMACEUTICS:

LACHMAN – chapter 1 to 7 are important. Chapter 8, 11 – 22 are to be done from this Tables on page number are important – 27, 37, 44, 98, 151, 165, 174, 321, 357 (only ingredients), 416 (only ingredients), 419, 434, 453, 463, 467, 508, 514, 515, 518, 521, 522, 551, 570 (names only), 621,631, 634, 642, 646 (tricky question like most permeable can be asked), 648. **MARTIN-** if you read Subramanyam whole, then do chapter 1, and last 2 chapters (biomaterials and delivery systems from it.)

BRAHMANKAR – whole book, read units of various parameters. CDDS. Remember various release models.

Cosmetics- remember only general things from B. M. Mitthal.

R. M Mehta – Posology, calculations are important.

COOPER-GUN – Read method for sterilization of various injections given at the end of book. Containers, surgical instruments and sterilization at least see if u get time.

EXTRA – stability testing, ICH guidelines, drug approval process like NDA, ANDA, ORANGE BOOK.

Intellectual property rights (NIPER only).

What is being studied in NIPER is also asked. (That leave to us) GMP guidelines.

PHARMACOLOGY:

- Rang and dale remains the standard book for GPAT/NIPER. (Do all important tables from it.)
- K.D TRIPATHI – see haematology, cancer, antibiotics, disinfectants and vaccines from it.
- See adverse drug reactions from ROGER-WALKER book.
- Clinical trials.
- Pharmacological classification from KDT only.

MEDICINAL CHEMISTRY:

- Wilson – read only following things:
- Structures of important drugs(s) and their starting material.

Important SAR related point:

- E.g. position responsible for acid instability of erythromycin. No of isomers for particular drug.
- Active isomer. Group responsible for activity of drug.
- Which class drug belongs?
- (Chemical class, not pharmacological. Pharmacological class from K.D TRIPATHI only)

<u>**Steroid chapter is very important.**</u>

IUPAC you can see of above drugs from Harkishan Singh book. Just see the structure u will notice how IUPAC is given for some of above drugs IUPAC Might be complex and lengthy or not found just leave it.

- Bioisosterism.
- QSAR – From FOYE/SN PANDYA.
- COMPFA like softwares.(NIPER) – LEAVE TO US
- IUPAC from Harkishan Singh book only.

PHARMACOGNOSY:

- Kokate remains the standard book.
- Whole book.
- BS, CC, synonym, use, adulterant, chemical test, substitute, structure (of imp drugs)
- If there are less adulterants or less info about adulterants in Kokate see Trease and Evans for further.
- Earlier chapters general introduction are important from Kokate.
- WHO guidelines – Kokate is good but with limited information. See other book.
- Biochemical pathways – remember starting points.
- Amino acids from which alkaloids are derived are to be remembered
- E.g tropane alkaloids from ornithine.
- Microscopy of following drugs:
- Read Khandelwall book other than above microscopies full.

ORGANIC CHEMISTRY

- Read only name reactions: Hoffman rearrangement etc.
- Mehta and Mehta or Morrison/Boyd
- Stereochemistry from (M/M or M/M).
- Various catalyst from M/M E.g lindlar catalyst, Wilkinson catalyst
- General concepts from – M/M
- Glossary of M/M

INORGANIC CHEMISTRY: Bahl and Tuli only –thermodynamic and nuclear pharmacy chapters are very important. Other chapters are also important.

- Chatwal – remember only common names of compounds and their use and water for injection limits.

MICROBIOLOGY

- Only Kokare (whole book) is enough.
- Vaccines read from it and also IP
- Something from Tortora (For NIPER– we will say later).

BIOCHEMISTRY

- Satyanarayan is enough:
- Do chapters 1 to 7 and metabolism chapters.
- Do all important tables.
- Biochemical teats (from R.K. GOYAL - available in GUJARAT only others students should see SATYANARAYAN AND KALE BOOK)

PHARMA ANALYSIS:

- Diagnostic tests.
- MASS – SILVERSTEIN, KASTURE, RAVISHANKAR.
- N – RAVISHANKAR, KASTURE, KEMP. (NIPER – PAVIA)
- UV, IR – RAVISHANKAR, KASTURE, CHATWAL/YR SHARMA.
- AAS/FLAME PHOTOMETRY/FLUORIMETRY – RAVISHANKAR, KASTURE.
- GRAVIMETRY/REDOX/ACID-BASE/POALRIMETRY/POLAROGRAPHY/
- CONDUCTOMETRY/AMPEROMETRY /ETC– RAVISHANKAR KASTURE.
- CALCULATIONS - UNDERWOOD.
- DSC/DTA/TGA – MARTIN, REMINGTON,
- KARL-FISCHER/KJELDAHL/CAURIUS/DUMAS etc determination methods - bahl and bahl or any other book.
- Assays- KASTURE OR RAVISHANKAR.

- See analysis part from /REMINGTON also.
- Circular dichronism.
- Chromatography – RAVISHANKAR/KASTURE.

JURISPRUDENCE

- GK JANI/ KUCHEKAR.
- Read important years.
- D and C act
- Schedules
- Form numbers
- Members
- Place of various institutes.

NIPER ONLY READ FOR NIPER BEFORE GPAT

- Biostatistics general concepts
- Management/accountancy/partnership: use Gujarat board 11 or 12 standard books like – accountancy, secretial practice etc. or what is studied in NIPER.
- Noble prize winners recent.
- Pharma news recent
- General knowledge.
- Aptitude (Maths)
- Recent approved USFDA DRUGS (do only approved in May/June/July – upto NIPER exam date)
- Banks full forms and when they established.
- Pharmaceutical full forms.
- Name and location of important institutes.
- Any other useful information which we say at last time.

GPAT 2021

STUDY MATERIAL

DRUGS AND THEIR ACTIVE METABOLITES

SR.NO.	DRUG	ACTIVE METABOLITE
1	Allopurinol	Oxipurinol (Alloxanthine)
2	Amytryptylline	Nortryptalline
3	Amphetamine	P-Methoxy Amphetamine
4	Carmapazepine	Carmapazemine-10,11-Eporide
5	Carbimazole	Thiamazole
6	Cephaloglycine	Desacetyl Cephaloglycine
7	Chloral Hydrate	Trichloroethanol
8	Chlordiazepoxide	7-hydroxy Chloropromazine
9	Chlorpromazine	7-hydroxy Chloropromazine
10	Chlorguanidine	Cyclogunal
11	Clofibrate	Free acid metabolite
12	Imipramine	N-oxide metabolite
13	Codeine	Morphine,Norcodeine
14	Diazepam	Oxazepam.N-Me-Oxazepam
15	Fenfluramine	Nor Fenfluramine
16	Guanethadine	N-Oxide
17	Lignocaine	N-Desmethyl metabolite
18	Morphine	Nor morphine
19	Naloxane	6--hydroxy Naloxane
20	Phenacetin	Paracetamol
21	Prednisone	Prednisolone
22	Premidone	Phenobarbitone
23	Spironolactone	Canrenone
24	Procainamide	N-Acetyl metabolite
25	Propanolol	N-deisopropyl met
26	Quinidine	3-Hydroxy quinine
27	Rifampicine	Desacetylated metabolite

28	Thioridazine	Mesoridazine

29	Trimethedione	Dimethedione
30	Warfarin	Warfarin alcohol
31	Vit D	1,2 Dihydroxy metabolite
32	Reserpine	Methyl reserpate

PRODUCTS AND ANIMALS USED FOR BIOASSAYS

SR	DRUG PRODUCT	ANIMAL
1	Digitalis	Pigeon
2	Glycogen	Cat
3	Insulin inj,	Rabbit
4	Oxytocin	Chicken
5	Parathyroid	Dog
6	Vasopressin	Rat
7	Posterior pituitary	Chicken
8	Tubocurarine chloride	Rabbit
9	Chorionic gonadotropin	Male rat
10	Cod liver oil	Rachitic rat
11	Heparin sodium	Sheep
12	Iron dextran injection	Microbial cultures
13	Antiseptic and disinfectant	Frog
14	Fungicides and Herbicides	Mouse
15	Diphtheria toxoid	Rat
16	Atropine	Rabbit
17	Insulin inj.	Guinea pig
18	Elastomeric closures Plastic containers	Guinea pig

RECOMENDE NEEDLE SIZE FOR VARIOUS INJECTIONS

INJECTIONS	GUAGE	LENGTH IN INCHES
INTRADERMAL	26G	¼ or 3/8
S.C	26G	½-¾
	25G	½-¾
	22G	1 ½
I.M	24G	¾-1
	23G	1
	22G	1
	20G	1 ½
I.V	22G	1-1/4-1 ½
	20G	1 ½

	DRUG	VARIETY
1	**SENNA**	
	Indian senna	*Cassia angustifolia*
	Alexandrian senna	*Cassia acutifolia*
	Dog senna	*Cassia obovata*
	Palthe senna	*Cassia auriculata*
2	**ALOE**	
	Cape Aloe	*Aloe ferox*
	Curcao Aloe	*Aloe barbadensis*
	Socotriene/ Zangibar aloe	*Aloe perryii*
3	**RHUBARB**	
	Indian Rhubarb	*Rheum emodi*
	Chinese Rhubarb	*Rheum webbianum*

DRUG AND THEIR SYNONYMS

SR.NO.	DRUG	SYNONYMS
1	Cinchona	Panama bark
2	Lanolin	Wool fat
3	Crowfig seeds	Nuxvomica
4	Deadly night shade	Atropa beladona
5	Digitalis purpuria	Foxglove
6	American podophyllum	May apple
7	Indian tragacanth	Gum karaya
8	Devil's dung	Asafoetida
9	Indian squill	Urgenia
10	Indian tobacco	Lobelia
11	Flax seeds	Linseed
12	Periwinkle	Vinca visea
13	Ashwagandha	Withania somnifera
14	Alexendrian senna	Cassia acutifolia
15	Tinevally senna	Cassia angustifolia
16	Dog senna	Cassia obovata
17	Pathe senna	Cassia auriculata
18	Acasia	Gum Arabica
19	Sterculia	Karaya
20	Agar	Japnese is linglass
21	Plantago	Psyllium
22	Starch	Amylum
23	Rhubarb	Rheam.emodi.(IND.Rhubarb)
24	Cascara	Purshiana,sacred barc
25	Discoria	Wild Yam
26	Glycerrhiza	Liquarice
27	Quillalia	Panama bark
28	Quassia	Bitter wool

29	Pale calicher	Gambier catechu
30	Blach caticher	Cutch
31	Castor oil	Ricinus oil
32	Arachis oil	Reauut oil
33	Linseed iol	Flax seed oil
34	Olive oil	Saled oil
35	Hydro carpno oil	Chanlmogra oil
36	Theobrona oil	Cocoa butter
37	Cinnamon	Chinese cassia
38	Saffron	Crocus
39	Colchicum	Autumn Crocus, Meadow saffron seeds
40	Nutmeg	Mygistica
41	Chenopodium	American wore
42	Lipstick tree	Annato tree, Bixin
43.	Clove	Caryo phylum

SR NO	NAME OF THE DRUG	SIDE EFFECTS
1	ACE Inhibitors	Dry Cough
2	Amphotericin-B	Nephrotoxicity
3	Ampicillin	Hypersensitivity
4	Androgen	Virilization
5	Antipsychotics	Sedation, Orthostatic hypotension, Tardive dyskinesia
6	Anti- TB	Hepatotoxicity
7	Aspirin (cox-I Inhibitors)	Hepatotoxicity

8	Atropine	Dryness of mouth, Blurred vision, Constipation

No.	Drug	Adverse Effect
9	Celecoxib, Valdecoxib (cox-II Inhibitors)	Hepatotoxicity
10	Chlorambucil	Alopecia
11	Chloramphenicol	Grey baby syndrome, Bone marrow depression
12	Chloroquine	Phototoxicity
13	Ciprofloxacin	Phototoxicity
14	Clofazimine	Pigmentation of skin, Discoloration of Urine
15	Clozapine	Agranulocytosis
16	Erythromyicin	Cholestatic Juandice
17	Ethambutol	Optic Neuritis, Retrobulbular Neuritis
18	Hydrochlorthiazide	Hypokalamia
19	Isoniazid	Peripheral Neurtis
20	Metronidazole	Disulfiram like reaction
21	Minoxidil	Hirsutism
22	Morphine	Constipation
23	Nimesulide	Hepatotoxicity
24	Nitrogen Mustard	Bone marrow depression
25	Nitroglycerin	Palpitation
26	Penicillin-G	Jarisch Heximer Reaction
27	Phenformin	Lactic acidosis, GI disturbance, Metalic taste
28	Phenytoin	Hirsutism
29	Quinidine	Cinchonism
30	Quinine Sulphate	Black Water Fever

31	Repaglinide	Althralgia
32	Rosaglitazone	Anemia,Weight gain
33	Sitagliptin	Coldness
34	Spironolactone	Hyperkalamia
35	Cimetidine	Gynacomastia
37	Sulfonyl Ureas derivatives	Bone marrow depression
38	Terfenadine	Type-I arrhythmia
39	Tetracyclines	Discoloration of teeth
40	Thalidomide	Phocomelia

CAPSULE NO & THEIR APPROXIMATE CAPACITY IN mg & ml

CAPSULE SIZE	Mg	Ml
000 (Largest)	950	1.37
00	650	0.95
0	450	0.68
1	300	0.50
2	250	0.37
3	200	0.30
4	150	0.21
5 (Smallest)	100	0.13

TYPE OF OIL	OIL: WATER: GUM RATIO
FIXED OILS	4:2:1
VOLATILE OILS	2:2:1
MINERAL OILS	3:2:1
OLEORESINS	1:2:1

CODE: **LPSO** (APPLY THIS FOR TWEENS & SPANS)

For eg. **SPANS 20** MEAN   SORBITAN MONO LAURATE

TWEEN 80 MEAN   POLYOXYETHYLENE SORBITAN

MONOOLEATE

❖ **L** : LAURATE - 20

- ❖ **P** : PALMITATE - 40
- ❖ **S** : STEARATE - 60
- ❖ **O** : OLEATE - 80

SOLUBILITY

Descriptive Term	Approx. Vol of Solvent in ml/gm of Solute
Very soluble	less than 1
Freely soluble	1 to 10
Soluble	10 to 30
Sparingly soluble	30 to 100
Slightly soluble	100 to 1000
Very slightly soluble	1000 to 10,000
Practically insoluble	more than 10,000

STORAGE TEMPERATURE

COLD TEMPERATURE	2 to 8 degree centigrade
COOL TEMPERATURE	8 to 25
ROOM TEMPERATURE	Prevailing in the working area
WARM TEMPERATURE	Between 30 to 40
EXCESSIVE HEAT	> 40 degree

SUCROSE BASED DILUANTS

DIPAC	97 % sucrose + 3% moddified dextrose
NUTAB	95 % sucrose + 4 % invert sugar
SUGAR TAB	90 - 93 % sucrose + 7 - 10 % invert sugar

Carr's index

The bulk density was the quotient of weight to the volume of the sample. Tapped density was determined as the quotient of weight of the sample to the volume after tapping a measuring cylinder for 500 times from a height of 2 inch. The Carr's index (percentage compressibility) was calculated as one hundred times the ratio of the difference between tapped density and bulk density to the tapped density.

% Carr's Index = (Tapped density – Bulk density) / Tapped density * 100
% Carr's Index = $(T_D - B_D) / T_D * 100$

Hausner's Ratio

Hausner's Ratio = Tapped density / Bulk density	H.R = T_D / B_D

Hausner's ratio is the ratio of tapped density to the bulk density.

% CI	FLOW CHARACTER	HAUSNER RATIO
< or = 10	Excellent	1 - 1.11
11 – 15	Good	1.12 - 1.18
16 – 20	Fair	1.19 - 1.25
21 – 25	passable	1.26 - 1.34
26 – 31	poor	1.35 - 1.45
32 – 37	very poor	1.46 - 1.59
>38	very very poor	> 1.6

Angle of repose

The angle of repose is a relatively simple technique for estimating the flow properties of a powder. It can easily be determined by allowing a powder to flow through a funnel and fall freely onto a surface. The height and diameter of the resulting cone are measured and the angle of repose calculated from this equation:

Tan Ø = h/r

Where, '**h**' is the height of the powder cone and '**r**' is the radius of the powder cone.

ANGLE OF REPOSE	FLOW CHARACTER
25 – 30	Excellent
31 – 35	Good
36 – 40	Fair

41 – 45	Passable
46 – 55	Poor
56 – 65	Very Poor
>66	Very Very Poor

TYPES OF GLASS USED IN PHARMACEUTICAL INDUSTRIES

Parenteral Use

- Type I Glass:
  - Highly Resistant Borosillicate.
  - Used for Buffered and Unbuffered aqueous solution.
- Type II Glass:
  - Highly Resistant Sodalime glass.
  - Buffered aqueous solution below pH 7.0
- Type III Glass:
  - Moderately Resistant Sodalime glass.
- Non-Parenteral Use
  - Type IV Glass:
  - General Purpose Sodalime glass.
  - Not for parenteral, for tablet, liquid oral and externals.
  - Used for dry powder and oily solution.

ANTIDOTES FOR SOME DRUGS

SR NO	DRUG NAME	ANTIDOTE
1	Acetaminophen	NAC (N-acetyl-L-cysteine) dosage
2	Alcohols (ethylene glycol, methanol)	IV ethanol, fomepizol (potent inhibitor of ADH)
3	Heparin	Protamine
4	Warfarin	vitamin k
5	Antidepressants	
	TCA's	benzodiazepines, phenytoin, physiostigmine

		SSRI's	Cycloheptadine
6	Benzodiazepines	Flumazenil
7	Beta antagonists	glucagon and epinephrine
8	Calcium antagonists	calcium, glucagon, insuline & dextrose combination
9	Cocaine	BZD's for seizuries; labetalol for hypertension; Neuroleptics for psychosis
10	Cyanide	amyl nitrite; sodium nitrite; sodium thio sulphate
11	Digoxin	Digibind
12	Electrolytes	
	a.Magnesium	10%CaCl2 temp to antagonize cardiac effects of Mg
	b.Potassium-	10%CaCl2 10%; NaHCO3(causes intracellular shift of pot);
13	Iron	deferoxamine (chelate iron)
14	Isoniazid	pyridoxine (reverses INH induced seizures)
15	Lead	Ca Disodium EDTA ; BAL (dimercaprol)
16	Lithium	no effective treatment
17	Opiates	naloxone; nalmefene
18	Organophosphates	atropine; pralidoxamine
19	Salicylates	activated charcoal
20	Theophylline	charcoal; beta antagonists
21	glucose & Insulin (Intracellular shift of pot.)	sodium polystyrene sulfonate (cationic exchange resin)

SYNONYMS AND THEIR COMMON NAMES

SR NO	SYNONYM	COMMON NAME
1	Rochelle salt	Sodium Potassium Tartarate
2	Dakin's solution	Sodium Hypochloride
3	Glaubers salt	Sodium Sulphate
4	Epsom salt	Magnesium Sulphate
5	China clay	Heavy Kaolin
6	Gypsum	Calcium Sulphate
7	Calomel	Mercurous Chloride
8	Soap clay	Bentonite
9	French chalk	Talc
10	Alum	Potassium Aluminium Sulphate
11	Hypo	Sodium Thiosulphate
12	Precipitated chalk	Calcium Carbonate
13	Slaked lime	Calcium Hydroxide
14	Bleaching powder	Chlorinated Lime
15	Burrows solution	Aluminium Acetate Solution
16	Laughing gas	Nitrous Oxide
17	Tear gas (CS gas)	Chlorobenzylidine Malononitrile
18	Iodine tincture	Weak Iodine Solution
19	knock out drops	Chloral Hydrate
20	Washing soda	Sodium carbonate
21	Baking soda	Sodium bicarbonate
22	Costic soda	Sodium hydroxide
23	Lugols solution	Aqueous Iodine Solution

VACCINES

LIVE ATTENUATED:	INACTIVATED	RECOMBINANT:
MEASLES	RABIES	HEPATITIS B
MUMPS	INFLUENZA	
POLIO	TETANUS	TOXOID:
RUBELLA	HEPATITS A	DIPTHERIA
TYPHOID		TETANUS
VARICELLA		
TUBERCULOSIS		
YELLOWFEVER		

TEST ORGANISM FOR MICROBIOLOGICAL ASSAY OF ANTIBIOTIC

SR NO	ANTIBIOTIC	TEST ORGANISM
1	Amikacin	*Staphlococcus aureus*
2	Amphotericin B	*Saccharomyces cerevisiae*
3	Bacitracin	*Micrococcus luteus*
4	Bleomycin	*Mycobacterium smegmatis*
5	Carbenicillin	*Pseudomonas aeruginosa*
6	Doxycycline	*Staphlococcus aureus*
7	Erythromycin	*Micrococcus luteus*
8	Framycetin	*Bacillus pumilis , staphylococcus aureus*
9	Gentamycin	*Staphylococcus epidermidis*
10	Kanamycin	*Bacillus pumilis, staphylococcus aureus*
11	kanamycin B	*Bacilus subtilis*
12	Neomycin	*Staphlococcus epidermidis*
13	Novobiocin	*Staphlococcus epidermidis*
14	Nystatin	*Saccharomyces cerevisiae*
15	Oxyteracycline	*Bacillus cereus, Staphylococcus aureus*
16	Polymyxin B	*Bordetella bronchiseptica*

17	Rifamycin	*Bacillus subtilis*
18	Streptomycin	*Bacillus subtilis , Klebsiella pneumonia*
19	Tetracycline	*Bacillus cereus, Staphylococcus aureus*

DISEASE ASSOCIATED WITH ALTERED NEUROTRANSMITTERS LEVELS IN BRAIN

SR NO	DISEASE	NEUROTRANSMITTERS LEVELS
1	Parkinsonism	Decreased DOPAMINE in striatum
2	Schizophrenia	Increased DOPAMINE levels
3	Depression	Decreased NOREPINEPHRINE & 5-HT
4	Mania	Decreased NOREPINEPHRINE & 5-HT
5	Hallucination	Increased 5-HT
6	Alzheimer's	Decreased ACETYLCHOLINE & Destruction of Cholinergic Neurons
7	Athetosis	Decreased GABA in Putamen
8	Chorea	Decreased GABA in Caudate Nucleus
9	Amyotropic lateral sclerosis	Decreased ACETYLCHOLINE

ENZYMES AND THEIR METAL COFACTORS

FE2+	CYTOCHROMEOXIDASE, CATALASE, PEROXIDASE
CU2+	CYTOCHROME OXIDASE
ZN2 +	DNA POLYMERASE, CARBONIC ANHYDRASE, ALCOHOL DEHYDROGENASE
MG2 +	HEXOKINASE, GLUCOSE 6 PHOSPHATE
MN2+	ARGINASE
K+	PYRUVATE KINASE
NI2+	UREASE
MO	NITRATE REDUCTASE

SE	GLUTATHIONE PEROXIDASE

MICROSOMAL ENZYMES INDUCERS AND INHIBITORS

MICROSOMAL ENZYME INDUCERS
ALCOHOL
CHLORALHYDRATE
CORTISONE

NICOTINE
PREDNISOSLONE
PHENYTOIN
CHLORDIAZEPOXIDE
IMIPRAMINE
PHENOBARBITAL
TESTOSTERONE

MICROSOMAL ENZYME INHIBITORS
ALLOPURINOL
ORAL ANTIDIABETICS
DISULFIRAM
METRONIDAZOLE
ORAL ANTICOAGULANTS
ANABOLIC AGENTS
CHLORAMPHENICOL
ISONIAZID
MONOAMINE OXIDASE INHIBITORS
CEMETIDINE

DISEASE	DEFECTIVE ENZYME
ALBINISM -	TYROSINE-3-MONO OXYGENASE
ALKAPTONURIA	- HOMOGENTISATE1,2-DIOXYGENASE

GALACTOSEMIA -	GALACTOSE-1-PHOSPHATE IRIDYLYL TRANSFERASE
HOMOCYSTINURIA -	CYSTATHIONE B- SYNTHASE
PHENYLKETONURIA -	PHENYLALANINE-4-MONO OXYGENASE
TAYSACHS DISEASE	- HEXOSAMINIDASE A
HYPERVALINEMIA	- VALINE TRANSAMINASE
ARGINOSUCCINIC -	ARGINOSUCCINATE LYASE ACIDEMIA
KRABBES DISEASE -	BETA GALACTOSIDASE

FABRYS DISEASE -	ALPHA GALACTOSIDASE
NIEMANN PICK DISEASE -	SPHINGOMYELINASE
FARBERS DISEASE -	CERAMIDASE
GAUCHERS DISEASE -	BETA GLUOSIDASE

DIAGNOSTIC TESTS

NAME OF DISEASE	DIAGNOSTIC TESTS
SYPHILIS	VDRL TEST, KAHN TEST, WASSERMAN TEST TREPONEMA IMMOBILIZATION TEST, FLUROESCENT ANTIBODY-ABSORBED SERUM TEST.
DIPTHERIA	SCHICK TEST, ELEX TEST
T.B	TUBERCULIN, MANTOUX TEST
LEPROSY	LEPROMIN TSEST
TYPHOID OR ENETRIC FEVER	WIDAL TEST
RHUMETOID ARTHRITIS	ROSE WATER TEST
SMALL POX	OUCHTERLONY

PNEUMONIA	COLD HEMAGLUTINATION TEST, STREPTOCOCCUS MG HEMAGLUTINATION TEST
BRUCELLOSIS-	COOMBS TEST(OPSONIZATION TEST)
LYMPHOGRANULOMA VENERUM	FREI TEST
TYPHUS FEVER-	WEIL FELIX TEST

HEMOPHILLIUS-	DUCREY TEST
SCARLET FEVER-	DICK TEST
TO DETECT HUMAN CHORNIC GONADOTROPHIN IN SERUM OF WOMAN	RADIO IMMUNO ASSAY(RIA)

BIOASSAYS OF DRUGS AND ITS EFFECT ON THE ANIMAL

ADRENALINE	BP raising effects in spinal cats
NORADRENALINE	BP raising effects in spinal cats
HISTAMINE	Contraction of isolated guinea pig ileum
INSULIN	Hypoglycemic convulsions in mice
ACETYLCHOLINE	Contraction of isolated frog rectus muscle
D TC	Rabbit head drop due to paralysis of neck muscles
DIGITALIS	Death due to cardiac arrest in guinea pig
OXYTOCIN	Contraction of guinea pig uterine muscles
ANDROGENS	Growth copons comb
ADRENO CORTICO TROPIC HORMONE	Adrenal ascorbic acid estimation in hypophysectomised rats

MICRO ORGANISMS USED AS BIOASSAYS FOR VITAMINS

ASSAY MICRO ORGANISM	VITAMIN
Lactobacillus casei	BIOTIN, FOLICACID, PYRIDOXAL, RIBOFLAVINE
L. Arabinosus	CALCIUM PANTOTHENATE, NICOTINIC ACID
L.leichmanii	CYANOCOBALAMIN
L.viridans	THIAMINE
Saccharomyces urarum	INOSITOL
Acetobacter suboxydans	PANTHOTHENOL
Neurospora crassa (or) s.carlsberginsis	PRIDOXINE

BIOLOGICAL INDICATORS

Moist heat sterilisation (121 degre Centi)	*Bacillus stearo thermophilus*
Dry heat sterilisation (160 degre centi)	*Bacillus subtilis var niger*
Hydrogen peroxide and peracetic acid	*Bacillus stearo thermophilus*
Ethylene oxide , formaldehyde	*Bacillus subtilis var niger*
Ionising radiation	*Bacillus pumilis*

TESTS AND THEIR USES

SR NO	TEST	IDENIFY
1	Watson Schwartz Test	Urobilinogen
2	Schumms Test	Heme
3	Carrprice Test	Vit A
4	Gmelins Test	Bile Pigments
5	Gothlin Test	Scurvy

6	Gofmann Test	Serum Cholesterol
7	Murexide Test	Uric Acid
8	Reinsch Test	Heavy Metals
9	Gordons Test	Spinal Fluid
10	Biuret Test	Peptides
11	Legals Test	For Estimation Of Acetone
12	Ames Test	Carcinogenicity

SHORT CUTS FOR GPAT AND NIPER (EASY TO REMEMBER)

Busulfan feature: ABCDEF

- ❖ Alkylating agent
- ❖ Bone marrow suppression
- ❖ CML Indication
- ❖ Dark skin(hyperpigmentation)
- ❖ Endocrine insufficiency(adrenal)
- ❖ Fibrosis

Drugs causing Torsades de Pointes: APACHE

- ❖ Amiodarone
- ❖ Procainamide
- ❖ Arsenium
- ❖ Cisapride
- ❖ Haloperidol
- ❖ Erythromycin

Morphine side effects: MORPHINE

- ❖ Myosis
- ❖ Out of It (sedation)
- ❖ Respiratory depression
- ❖ Pneumonia(aspiration)
- ❖ Hypotension
- ❖ Infrequency (constipation,urinary retention)
- ❖ Nausea
- ❖ Emesis

Aspirin side effects: ASPIRIN

- Asthma
- Salicylism
- Peptic ulcer disease/phosphorylation-oxidat
- ion uncoupling/platelet disaggregation
- Intestinal blood loss
- Reye's Syndrome
- Idiosyncracy
- Noise(tinnitus)

SSRIs side effects: SSRI

- Seratonin syndrome
- Stimulate CNS
- Reproductive disfunction in male
- Insomnia

Inhalation anesthetics: SHINE

- Sevoflane
- Halothane
- Isoflurane
- Nitrous oxide
- Enflurane

Teratogenic drugs:"Win Teratogenic"

- Warfarin
- Thalidomide

Epileptic drugs:

- Phenytoin,
- Valproate,
- Amazepine
- Retinoid
- ACE inhibitor

Third element: Lithium

Gynaecomastia causing drugs: DISCOS

- ❖ Digoxin
- ❖ Isoniazid
- ❖ Spironolactone
- ❖ Cimetidine
- ❖ Oestrogens
- ❖ Stilboestrol

Methyldopa Side effects: METHYLDOPA

- ❖ Mental retardation
- ❖ Electrolyte imbalance
- ❖ Tolerance
- ❖ Headache/ Hepatotoxicity
- ❖ Psychological upset
- ❖ Lactation in female
- ❖ Dry mouth
- ❖ Oedema
- ❖ Parkinsonism

Antirheumatic agents: CHAMP

- ❖ Cyclophosphamide
- ❖ Hydroxycloroquine and choloroquinine
- ❖ Auranofin and other gold compounds
- ❖ Methotrexate
- ❖ Penicillamine

Phenytoin: adverse effects PHENYTOIN

- ❖ P-450 interactions
- ❖ Hirsutism
- ❖ Enlarged gums
- ❖ Nystagmus
- ❖ Yellow-browning of skin
- ❖ Teratogenicity
- ❖ Osteomalacia
- ❖ Interference with B12 metabolism (hence anemia)

- ❖ Neuropathies: vertigo, ataxia, and headache

<u>Sodium Valproate side effccts VALPROATE</u>

- ❖ Vomiting
- ❖ Alopecia
- ❖ Liver toxicity
- ❖ Pancreatitis/ Pancytopenia
- ❖ Retention of fats (weight gain)
- ❖ Oedema (peripheral oedema)
- ❖ Appetite increase
- ❖ Tremor
- ❖ Enzyme inducer (liver)

<u>Amiodarone: action, side effects: 6 P's:</u>

- ❖ Prolongs action potential duration
- ❖ Photosensitivity
- ❖ Pigmentation of skin
- ❖ Peripheral neuropathy
- ❖ Pulmonary alveolitis and fibrosis
- ❖ Peripheral conversion of T4 to T3 is inhibited -> hypothyroidism

<u>Antiparkinson Drugs: SALAD</u>

- ❖ Selegiline
- ❖ Anticholinenergics (trihexyphenidyl, benzhexol, ophenadrine)
- ❖ L-Dopa + peripheral decarboxylase inhibitor (carbidopa, benserazide)
- ❖ Amantadine
- ❖ Dopamine postsynaptic receptor agonists (bromocriptine, lisuride, pergolide)

<table>
<tr><td align="center">Therapeutic Index Formula
TILE TI = LD / ED</td></tr>
</table>

<u>Anti epeleptic drugs Dr.BHAISAB's New PC.</u>

- ❖ Deoxy barbiturates
- ❖ Barbiturates
- ❖ Hydantoin

- ❖ Aliphatic carb acids
- ❖ Iminostilbenes
- ❖ Succinimides
- ❖ BZD's
- ❖ Newer drugs
- ❖ Phenyltriazines
- ❖ Cyclic GABA analogues

Adverse effects of Tetracyclines-KAPIL DEV

- ❖ Kidney toxicity
- ❖ Antianabolic effect
- ❖ Phototoxicity
- ❖ Liver toxicity
- ❖ Diabetes insipidus

CAPTOPRIL Side effects CAPTOPRIL

- ❖ Cough Angioedema
- ❖ Agranulocystosis
- ❖ Proteinuria/ Potassium excess
- ❖ Taste changes
- ❖ Orthostatic hypotension
- ❖ Pregnancy contraindication/ Pancreatitis/ Pressure drop (first dose hypertension)
- ❖ Renal failure (and renal artery stenosis contraindication)/ Rash
- ❖ Indomethacin inhibition
- ❖ Leukopenia/Liver toxicity

Lithium: side effects LITH

- ❖ Leukocytosis
- ❖ Insipidus [diabetes insipidus, tied to polyuria]
- ❖ Tremor/ Teratogenesis
- ❖ Hypothyroidism

Myocardial Infarction (MI): signs and symptoms PULSE

* Persistent chest pains
* Upset stomach
* Lightheadedness
* Shortness of breath
* Excessive sweating

MI: basic management BOOMAR

* Bed rest
* Oxygen
* Opiate
* Monitor
* Anticoagulate
* Reduce clot size

Treatment of Heart Failure: ABCDE

* ACE inhibitors
* Beta-blockers
* Calcium channel blockers
* Diuretics
* Endothelin-converting enzyme inhibitors

Essential Amino acids

My True Love Is Through Valentine Love Phrases

* Methionine
* Threonine
* Leucine
* Isoleucine
* Tryptophan
* Valine
* Lysine
* Phenyl alanine

BLOOD GROUP AND ITS COLOR OF LABEL MOST IMP

BLOOD GROUP	COLOR OF LABEL
O	BLUE
A	YELLOW
B	PINK
AB	WHITE

ABBREVIATIONS IMP FOR GPAT AS WEL AS IN NIPER

Description of some Important Abbreviations:-

ABBREVIATIONS	FULL FORM
AAAS	American Association of Advancement of Science
AALAS	American Association for Laboratory Animal Science
AIOPI	Association of Information Officers of the Pharmaceutical Industry
ALF	American Liberation Front
ANDA	Abbreviated New Drug Application
BEA	Breeding for Experimental Animals
BINAS	Biosafety Information Network and Advisory Service
BMA	British Medical Association
BMJ	British Medical Journal
BPC	Bulk Pharmaceutical Chemicals
BPI	British Pharmaceutical Index
BrAPP	British Association of Pharmaceutical Physicians
BUAV	British Union for the Abolition of Vivisection
CADD	Computer Aided Drug Design
CDC	Centre for Disease Control
CIOMS	Council for International Organisations of Medical Sciences
CPCSEA	Committee for Purpose of Control & Supervision of Experimental Animals

CPI	Consumer Price Index
CRA	Clinical Research Associate
CRC	Clinical Research Council
CRF	Case Report Form
CRN	Clinical Research Network
CRO	Contract Research Organisation
CSM	Committee on Safety of Medicines
CTA	Clinical Trial Authorisation (formerly the CTX, CTC, DDX)
CTC	Clinical Trial Certificate (Now CTA)
CTC	Clinical Trials Centre
CTD	Common Technical Document
CTX	Clinical Trial Exemption (Now CTA)
DRA	Drug Regulatory Affairs
DUMP	Disposal of Unwanted Medicines and Poisons
EFPIA	European Federation of Pharmaceutical Industries & Associations
EMEA	European Medicine Agency
FDA	Food & Drug Administration
FIP	International Pharmaceutical Federations
GCP	Good Clinical Practices
GLP	Good Laboratory Practices
GMP	Good Manufacturing Practices
Gxp	Generic term for good practice requirements in the Pharmaceutical Industry
HIS	Indian Health Services
HPLC	High Performance Liquid Chromatography
HRSA	Health Resources & Service Administration
IACUC	Institutional Animal Care and Use Committee
IAES	Institutional Animal Ethics Committee

ICDRA	International Conference for Drug Regulatory Authorities
ICH	International Conference on Harmonization of technical requirement for registration of pharmaceuticals
IIG	Inactive Ingredient Guide
IMP	Investigational Medicinal Products IMP - Investigational Medicinal Products
IMPD	Investigational Medicinal Product Dossier
INDA	Investigational New Drug Application
INN	International non-proprietary names (for pharmaceutical substances)
INTDIS	International Drug Information System - the previous WHO adverse reactions database
IPC	Indian Pharmaceutical Congress
IPGA	Indian Pharmacy Graduate Association
ISO	International Organization for Standardization
ISoP	International Society of Pharmacovigilance
ISPE	International Society for Pharmacoepidemiology
MedDRA	Medical Dictionary for Drug Regulatory Affairs
NAFDAC	National Agency for Food and Drug Administration and Control, Nigeria
NCPA	National Community of Pharmacist Association
NCPO	National Conference of Pharmaceutical Organisations
NDA	New Drug Application
NDMS	National Disaster Medical System
NME	New Molecule Entity
NSAID	Non-Steroidal Anti-Inflammatory Drug

OTC	Over-The-Counter
PDS	Pharmacoepidemiology and Drug Safety (journal)
PEM	Prescription Event Monitoring
PHRMA	Pharmaceutical Research and Manufacturers Association
PIL	Package Insert Leaflet
PMDA	Pharmaceuticals and Medical Devices Agency, Japan
PMS	Post-Marketing Surveillance
POM	Prescription Only Medicine
PSM	Procurement and Supply Management
PSUR	Periodic Safety Update Report
QA	Quality Assurance
QSM-WHO	Quality Assurance and Safety of Medicines (WHO)
R&D	Research and Development
RAPS	Regulatory Affairs Professionals Society
RCT	Randomised Clinical Trials
RDE	Remote Data Entry
RDS	Research Defence Society
REC	Research Ethics Committee
RGN	Registered General Nurse
RPSGB	Royal Pharmaceutical Society of Great Britain
RSM	Royal Society of Medicine
Rx	Prescription (YOU TAKE)
SARS	Severe Acute Respiratory Syndrome
SCDM	Society for Clinical Data Management
SIDS	Sudden Infant Death Syndrome
SIGAR	Special Interest Group on Adverse Reactions
TGA	Therapeutic Goods Administration, Australia
TMF	Trial Master File
TUFAM	General Directorate of Pharmaceuticals and Pharmacy, Turkey

UDV	Unit Dose Vial
UKECA	United Kingdom Ethics Committee Authority
USP	United States Pharmacopoeia
WIPO	World Intellectual Patent Office

SCHEDULES	THE RULES
A	Perform for application for the licences, issues and renewal of licences, for sending memoranda under the Act.
B	Rates of fee for test or analysis by the Central Drugs Laboratory or the Government analysist.
C	List of biological and other special products whose import, sale, distribution and manufacturing are a governed by special provision.
C1	List of other special products whose import, sale, distribution and manufacturing are governed by special provision.
D	List of drugs exempted from the provisions of import of drugs.
E1	List of poisionous substances under the Ayurvedic (including Sidha) and Unani systems of medicine.
F & F1	Provisions applicable to the production, testing, storage, packing and labeling of biological and other Special products.
F2	Standards for surgical dressings.
F3	Standards for sterilized umbilical tapes.
FF	Standards of ophthalmic preparations.
G	List of substances that are required to be used only under medical supervision and which are to be labeled accordingly.

H	List of prescription drugs.
J	Disease or ailments which a drug may not purport to prevent or cure.
K	Drugs exempted from certain provision relating to manufacture of drugs.
M	GMP requirement of factory premises, plants and equipment.
M1	Requirement of factory premises etc. for manufacture of homoeopathic preparation.
M2	Requirement of factory premises etc. for manufacture of cosmetics.
N	List of minimum equipment for efficient running of a pharmacy.
O	Standard for disinfectant fluid.
P	Life period of drug.
Q	List of coals tar color permitted to be used in cosmetics.
R	Standard for mechanical contraceptive. CONDOMS
S	Standard for cosmetics.
T	Requirement of factory premises and hygienic condition for Ayurvedic (including Sidha) and Unani drugs.
U	Particulars to be shown in manufacturing, raw material and analytical records of drug.
U1	Particulars to be shown in manufacturing, raw material and analytical records of cosmetics.
V	Standard for patent or proprietary medicines.
W	List of drugs to be marketed under generic names only.
X	List of drugs whose import, manufacture and sale, labeling and packaging are governed by special provision.
Y	Requirement and guideline on clinical trials for import and manufacture of new drug.

<u>BETA BLOCKERS</u>

<u>Comparative information Pharmacological differences Agents with intrinsic sympathomimetic action (ISA)</u>

- ❖ Acebutolol,
- ❖ Carteolol,
- ❖ Celiprolol
- ❖ Mepindolol
- ❖ Oxprenolol
- ❖ Pindolol

<u>Agents with greater aqueous solubility (hydrophilic beta blockers)</u>

- ❖ Atenolol
- ❖ Celiprolol
- ❖ Nadolol,
- ❖ Sotalol

<u>Agents with membrane stabilizing effect</u>

- ❖ Acebutolol,
- ❖ Betaxolol,
- ❖ Pindolol,
- ❖ Propranolol

<u>Agents with antioxidant effect</u>

- ❖ Carvedilol,
- ❖ Nebivolol

INDICATION DIFFERENCES

<u>Agents specifically indicated for cardiac arrhythmia</u>

- ❖ Esmolol,
- ❖ Sotalol,
- ❖ Landiolol

<u>Agents specifically indicated for congestive heart failure</u>

- ❖ Bisoprolol,
- ❖ Carvedilol,
- ❖ Sustained-release metoprolol,

❖ Nebivolol

Agents specifically indicated for glaucoma

❖ Betaxolol,

❖ Carteolol,

❖ Levobunolol,

❖ Metipranolol,

❖ Timolol

Agents specifically indicated for myocardial infarction

❖ Atenolol,

❖ Metoprolol,

❖ Propranolol

Propranolol is the only agent indicated for control of tremor, portal hypertension, and esophageal variceal bleeding, and used in conjunction with α blocker therapy in phaeochromocytoma.

Agents specifically indicated for migraine prophylaxis

❖ Timolol,

❖ Propranolol

SOME IMP PH VALUE

Blood:	7.4
Tear	7.2
Skin	7.4
Secretion of Skin:	5.5
Gastric juice:	Infants: 5, Adults: 2
Saliva:	6.3-6.7
Urine:	4.4-8
Stool:	approx. 6
Bile Juice:	8-8.6
Semen:	7.2-8
Vagina:	3.8-4.5

<u>MECHANISM OF ACTION</u>

1- **DNA Dependent RNA Polymerase**- Rifampcin

2- **RNA Dependent DNA Polymerase**- Zidovudine

3- **Proetin Synthesis Blocker**- Erythromycin, Chloramphenicol & Tetracycline

4- **ACE Inhibitor**- Captopril

5- **Ca Channel Blocker**- Nifedipine, Diltiazem

6- **COX Inhibitor**- Asprin

7- **GABA Facilitator**- Benzodiazepines

8- **Antimetabolites**- Methotrexate

9- **Loop Diuretics**- Frusemide

10- **High Ceiling Diuretics**- Spironolactone

11- **Alteration of bacterial DNA**- Choloroquine

12- **Inhibition of Viral replication**- Amantidine, Acyclovir

13- **H1 blocking agent**- Mepyramine, Loratadine

14- **H2 Blocking agent**- Rantidine, Cimetidine, Famotidine, Cyprohaptidine

15- **Proton Pump inhibitor**- Omeprazole

16- **DNA Metabolism Inhibitors**- Quinacrine (Mepacrine)

17- **Spindle Poison**- Vinca, Griesofulvin

18- **Folic acid synthesis inhibitor**- DDS

19- **GABA Inhibitor**- Sodium Valproate

20- **DNA Synthesis Prevention** – Nalidixic Acid

21- **Prostaglandin Synthesis Inhibition**- Oxyphenbutazone, Ibuprofen

22- **Mycolic acid synthesis inhibition**- INH

23- **Folic acid antagonist-** MTX, PAS, DDS & Primethamine

24- **Desruption of DNA structure**- MNZ

25- **Inhibition of cell wall synthesis**- Beta lactam antibiotics (penicillin)

26- **Release of nor epinephrine**- Ephedrine

27- **Ergosterol Biosnythesis Inhibitors**- Clotrimazole, Miconalzole, Ketoconazole

28- **Ach esterase inhibitors**- Physostigmine, Neostigmine, Edrophonium, Metrifonate

29- **Reverse Transcriptase Inhibitors**- Stavudine, zidovudine

30-Inhibition of HIV Protease- Amepranavir

31-DNA Gyrase Inhibitor- Cinoxacin

32-Inhibition of DNA Polymerase-Gossypol

33-NMDA Receptor Antagonist- Amantadine, Ketamine, Dextromethorphan, Memantine & Nitrous Oxide

34-DNA intercalating agent- Daunorubicin, Doxorubicin, Ellipticin & Ethidium Bromide

35-Antim mitotic agent- Amphethenile

36-Alkylating agent- Thiotepa

37-Alpha receptor antagonist- Phentolamine

38-Beta receptor antagonist- Propanolol, Aplrenolol

39-Alpha receptor agonist- Norepinehrine

40- Beta receptor agonist- Isoproterenol & Salbutamol

41-DNA Adduct Formation- Procarbazine

42-Carbonic anhydrase inhibitor- Acetazolamide

43-Phosphodiestrase Inhibitor- Theophylline

44-Thrombin action prevention- Heparin

45-Xanthine oxidase inhibitor- Allopurinol

46-Cholinergic Blockade- Ipratropium

47- Adenosine Deaminase inhibitor- Crisnatapase

48- Immunomodulation- Imiquimod

49- Amino acid transfer interference- Econazole

50- Mast Cell Stabilization- Ketosifen

MUST DO THIS TABLE IMP FROM JURI

SR NO	ORGANISATION	LOCATION
1	BCG Vaccine Lab	Chennai
2	Central drug testing lab (CDTL)	Mumbai
3	Central drug Laboratory (CDL)	Kolkata
4	Central Drug Research Institute (CDRI)	Lucknow

5	Central Research Institute (CRI)	Kasauli
6	Indian Drug Manufactures Association (IDMA)	Mumbai
7	Indian Society of Blood Trensfusion & Immunoheamatology	Pune
8	Indian Veterinary Research Institute (IVRI)	Izatnagar
9	Central Indian Pharmacoepia Laboratory (CIPL)	Ghaziabad
10	National Plasma Fractionation Centre (NPFC)	Mumbai
11	National Institute for Communicable Disease (NICD)	New Delhi
12	Indian Institute for Virology (IIV)	Pune
13	Organization of Pharmaceutical Procedures	Mumbai
14	Dabur Research foundation	Ghaziabad
15	Institute of applied man power research	New Delhi
16	CD Testing Lab	Mumbai
17	Synthetic Drug Plant	Hyderabad
18	National Institute of Nutrition (NIN)	Hyderabad
19	National Brain Research Institute (NBRI)	Manesar (Gurgaon)

IMPORTANT PHARMACOLOGICAL TERMS:

Antagonism

–The opposition between 2 or more medications ex. narcotics and Naloxone

- **Bolus**

–A single, often large dose of a drug. Often the initial dose

- **Cumulative action**

–An increased effect caused by multiple doses of the same drug. Caused by buildup in the blood.

•**Hypersensitivity**

–A reaction to a drug that is more profound than expected and which often results in an exaggerated immune response

•**Idiosyncrasy**

–A reaction to a drug that is significantly different from what is expected

- **Indication**
  - The medical condition for which the drug has proven therapeutic value.
- **Parenteral**
  - Any route of administration other than the digestive tract
- **Pharmacodynamics**
  - Study of the mechanisms by which drugs act to produce biochemical or physiological changes in the body
- **Pharmacokinetics**
  - Study of how drugs enter the body, reach their site of action and are eliminated from the body.
- **Potentiation**
  - The enhancement of a drug's effect by another drug
  - Eg. Promethazine may enhance the effect of morphine; also alcohol and barbiturates
- **Refractory**
  - The failure of a patient to respond as expected to a certain medication
- **Synergism**
  - The combined action of 2 or more drugs that is greater than the sum of the 2 drugs acting independently.
- **Therapeutic Action**
  - The intended action of a drug given in an appropriate medical setting
- **Therapeutic Threshold**
  - The minimum amount of a drug that is required to cause the desired response
- **Therapeutic Index**
  - The difference between the therapeutic threshold and the amount of the drug considered to be toxic
  - Often referred to as Safe and Effective range.
- **Tolerance**
  - The decreased sensitivity or response to a drug that occurs after repeated doses

–Increased doses are required to achieve the desired effect

- **Untoward Effect**

–A side effect of a drug that is harmful to the patient

STERILIZATION OF MEDIA

In almost all cases, once a medium is made, it must be treated to eliminate any microorganisms contaminating containers, media ingredients, weighing papers, or other surfaces that come in contact with the medium. If this is not performed correctly, contaminates arise during incubation, making microbiological investigations impossible. Sterilization is defined as the inactivation (or removal) of all life forms (including the pseudo- life forms, viruses) in a specific area. Culture media must be made sterile without inactivating nutrients necessary for growth of the microorganism. Equipment and media used in the microbiology laboratory are most often sterilized using one of the methods outlined below.

Autoclaving - moist heat (121°C) under pressure (15-17 lb/in2)

Mode of action - coagulates proteins

Materials - heat stable items such as most culture media, glass and metal, but not plastics

Oven - dry heat (160°C for several hours)

Mode of action - coagulates proteins

Materials - glass and metals but not liquids nor plastics

Filtration - 0.22 to 0.45 µm pore size

Mode of action - prevents organisms from passing through the filter, but does allow viruses to pass so therefore not sterilization in true sense.

Materials - Solutions of heat sensitive compounds such as some amino acids, vitamins, sugars etc.

Radiation - ultraviolet light or gamma rays

Mode of action - damages nucleic acids

Materials - heat sensitive solids such as plastics, however effective on surfaces only

<u>**Gas - ethylene oxide**</u>

Mode of action - inactivates enzymes

Materials - heat sensitive solids such as some plastics.

Temperature Relationships

Microorganisms as a whole, are able to grow at a tremendous range of temperatures. Bacteria have been discovered growing near the Galopagos trench (a marine ocean vent) at temperatures of 110°C and in super-cooled foods as low as -12°C. The temperature range that a specific microorganism is able to grow at is thought to be limited by the activity of its enzymes and the fluidity of the membrane. Extreme temperatures either prevent enzymes from carrying out their reactions quickly enough (at low temperatures) or denature (inactivate) enzymes (at high temp and sometimes low temperatures). It is also possible that temperature has its effect by interfering with the fluidity of membranes, too fluid at high temperatures, frozen at low temperatures. Overly fluid membranes cannot maintain their intergrety and leak, frozen membrane cannot perform vital functions such as electron transport.

Microbes can be classified by their **optimum** temperature for growth.

Organisms having an optimum of <20°C are termed Psychrophiles.
Those that grow optimally from 20 to 45°C are called Mesophiles.
Microorganisms that have temperature optima of >45°C are termed Thermophiles.

It is possible for an organisms to have an optimum temperature in one classification, but be capable of growing at temperatures much above or below the optimum. For example, *Bacillus coagulans* is capable of growth at mesophillic temperatures, but will also grow at temperatures of 55-60°C. These organisms are termed facultative thermophiles.

Microorganisms will cease to grow below their optimum temperature, but frequently will survive in an inert state. In fact refrigeration or freezing of bacteria can have a preservative effect. Most microorganisms are killed above the optimum temperature.

SOME IMPORTANT NOTES FOR GPAT AND NIPER EXAM

Partition Coefficient:

OCTANOL: water partition coefficient often used in formulation development.

Q10 Method of Shelf Life Estimation:

Shelf life estimation

> **Arrhenius Equation:** log = k2\k1 = Ea (T2 − T1)\ 2.3 RT1T2

> Q10 = [K (T+10)]/KT =e [(Ea /R) ({1/T+10} {1/T}]

$$Q10 = e \{(Ea/R) [(1/T + 10) - (1/T)]\}$$

Shelf Life Estimates:

Q10 = 2 Lower limit

Q10 = 3 Average, best estimate Q10 = 4 Upper limit

t90 Equation for Shelf Life Estimates:

t90 (T2) = t90 (T1)/Q10 (Delta T/10).

Note: A "+" Delta T decreases shelf life and a "-" Delta T increases shelf life.

Sweetening Agents:

- ❖ Dextrose
- ❖ Mannitol
- ❖ Saccharin
- ❖ Sorbitol
- ❖ Sucrose

Preservative Utilization:

- ❖ • Benzoic acid/sodium benzoate
- ❖ • Alcohol
- ❖ • Phenylmercuric nitrate/acetate
- ❖ • Phenol
- ❖ • Cresol
- ❖ • Chlorobutanol
- ❖ • Benzalkonium chloride
- ❖ • Methyl paraben/propyl paraben

❖ •Others

<u>Alcohols</u>

Ethanol is useful as a preservative when it is used as a solvent. It needs a relatively high concentration (> 10%) to be effective.

Propylene glycol also used as a solvent in oral solutions and topical preparations. It can function as a preservative in the range of 15 to 30%. It is not volatile like ethanol.

<u>Acids</u>

→ **Benzoic acid** and **sorbic acid** have low solubility in water.

→ They are used in a concentration range from **0.1 % to 0.5%.**

Only the non-ionized form is effective and therefore its use is restricted to preparations with a pH below 4.5.

<u>Esters</u>

Parabens are esters (methyl, ethyl, propyl and butyl) of p-hydroxybenzoic acid.

→ They are used widely in pharmaceutical products

→ They are effective and stable over a pH range of **4 to 8.**

→ They are employed at concentrations up to about **0.2%.**

→ Frequently 2 esters are used in combination in the same preparation.

→ To achieve a higher total concentration

→ To be active against a wider range of microorganisms.

<u>Quaternary Ammonium Compounds</u>

❖ Benzalkonium chloride is used at a relatively low concentration **0.002 to 0.02%.**

❖ This class of compounds has an optimal activity over the pH range of 4 to 10 and is quite stable at most temperatures.

❖ Because of the cationic nature of this type of preservative it is incompatible with many anionic compounds.

<u>Antioxidants</u>

Vitamins, essential oils & almost all fats and oils can be oxidized.

Oxidation reaction can be initiated by:

1. **Heat:** maintain oxidizable drugs in a cool place

2. **Light:** use of light- resistant container

3. **Heavy metals** (e.g. Fe, Cu): effect of trace metals can be minimized by using citric acid or ethylenediamine tetraacetic acid (EDTA) i.e. sequestering agent.

   Antioxidants as propyl & octyl esters of gallic acid, tocopherols or vitamin E, sodium sulfite, ascorbic acid (vit. C) Can be used.

:<u>SWEETENING AGENTS</u>

Sucrose is the most widely used sweetening agent.

Advantages: Colourless, highly water soluble, stable over a wide pH range (4-8), increase the viscosity, masks both salty and bitter taste, has soothing effect on throat.

Polyhydric alcohols (sorbitol, mannitol and glycerol) possess sweetening power and can be used for diabetic preparations.

<u>Humectants:</u> such as glycerin and sorbitol (5-20% in MW)

❖ Increase the viscosity of the preparation

❖ Enhance the sweetness of the product

❖ Improve the preservative qualities of the product.

<u>Surfactants:</u> Non-ionic and anionic surfactants aid in the solubilization of flavors and in the removal of debris by providing foaming action. **Cationic surfactants such as cetylpyridinium chloride** are used for their antimicrobial properties, but these tend to impart a bitter taste.

<u>Flavours:</u> are used in conjunction with alcohol and humectants to overcome disagreeable tastes. The principle flavoring agents are **peppermint, cinnamon, menthol or methyl salicylate.**

<u>Otic Solutions:</u>

The main classes of drugs used for topical administration to the ear include local anesthetics, **e.g.:** benzocaine; antibiotics e.g.; neomycin; and anti-inflammatory agents, e.g.; cortisone.

Polyols (e.g. glycerin or sorbitol) may be added to

- retard crystallization of sucrose or increase the solubility of added ingredients.

<u>Invert sugar</u>

D is more readily fermentable than sucrose D tend to darken in color

C retard the oxidation of other substances.

The levulose formed during inversion is sweeter than sucrose; therefore the resulting syrup is sweeter than the original syrup.

<u>When syrup is overheated it caramelizes.</u>

<u>The sucrose in the 66.7% w/w solution must be at least 95% inverted.</u>

<u>MUCILAGES</u>

The official mucilages are thick viscid, adhesive liquids, produced by dispersing gum <u>(acacia or tragacanth)</u> in water.

Mucilages are used as suspending agents for insoluble substances in liquids; their colloidal character and viscosity prevent immediate sedimentation.

Synthetic agents e.g. carboxymethylcellulose (CMC) or polyvinyl alcohol are nonglycogenetic and may be used for diabetic patients.

ELIXIRS

Are clear, pleasantly flavored, sweetened hydroalcoholic liquids intended for oral use. They are used as flavors and vehicles

<u>E.g. Dexamethasone Elixir USP and Phenobarbital Elixir USP.</u>

COLLODIONS:

Are liquid preparations containing pyroxylin (a nitrocellulose) in a mixture of ethyl ether and ethanol

Rubefacient

A substance for external application that produces redness of the skin e.g. by causing dilation of the capillaries and an increase in blood circulation.

Counterirritant

A medicine applied locally to produce superficial inflammation in order to reduce deeper inflammation.

Effervescent tablet:

contain acid substances **(citric and tartaric acids) and carbonates or bicarbonates** and which react rapidly in the presence of water by releasing carbon dioxide.

Oxymels: These are preparations in which the vehicle is a mixture of acetic acid and honey.

Magnesium sulphate: Magnesium cause smooth muscle relaxation secondary to inhibition of calcium uptake.

Atopy is strongest predisposing factor for developing asthma.

Asthma is a **chronic inflammatory disorder of the airways** in which many **cells & cellular elements play a role** (Mast cells, eosinophils, T lymphocytes, macrophages, neutrophils, & epithelial cells).

Child-onset asthma

–Associated with **Atopy**

–**IgE** directed against common **environmental antigens**

(House-dust mites, animal proteins, fungi)

–**Viral wheezing** Infants/children, allergy/allergy history associated with **continuing asthma** through childhood.

Leukotriene modifiers:

- ❖ Zafirlukast - leukotriene receptor antagonist
- ❖ Zileuton - 5-lipoxygenase inhibitor is alternative therapy to low doses of inhaled steroids/nedocromil/cromolyn. 5-lipoxygenase inhibitor

Long-acting beta2-agonists (LABA)

Beta2-receptors are the predominant receptors in bronchial smooth muscle Stimulate ATP- cAMP which leads to relaxation of bronchial smooth muscle and inhibition of release of mediators of immediate hypersensitivity Inhibits release of mast cell mediators such as histamine, leukotrienes, and prostaglandin-D2. Beta1-receptors are predominant receptors in heart, but up to 10-50% can be beta2-receptors.

Long-acting beta2-agonists (LABA)

- ☐ Salmeterol (Serevent)

- Salmeterol with fluticasone (Advair).
- Albuterol

DRUGS AND SCHEDULE

Schedule I

Drugs in this schedule have a high abuse potential (narcotic and hallucination effects). Examples are **heroin, marijuana.**

Schedule II

Drugs in this schedule have a high abuse potential with severe psychic or physical dependence liability. Included are certain narcotic analgesics, stimulants, and depressant drugs. Examples are opium, morphine, codeine, hydromorphone, methadone, meperidine, oxycodone, anileridine, cocaine,amphetamine,methamphetamine, phenmetrazine, methylphenidate, amobarbital, pentobarbital, secobarbital, methaqualone, and phencyclidine.

Schedule III

Drugs in this schedule have an abuse potential less than those in Schedules I and II and include compounds containing limited quantities of certain narcotic analgesic drugs, and other drugs such as barbiturates, glutethimide, methyprylon, and chlorphentemine. Any suppository dosage form containing amobarbital, secobarbital, or pentobarbital is in this schedule.

Schedule IV

Drugs in this schedule have an abuse potential less than those listed in Schedule III and include such drugs as barbital, phenobarbital, chloral hydrate, ethchlorvynol, meprobabmate, chlordizepoxide, diazepam, oxazepam, chloroazepate, flurazepam, etc.

Schedule V

Drugs in this schedule have an abuse potential less than those listed in Schedule IV and consist primarily of preparations containing limited quantities of certain narcotic analgesic drugs used for **antitussive and antidiarrheal** purposes.

<u>**SOME IMP PONTS FROM PHARMACEUTICS**</u>

Creams – semisolid emulsion systems (o/w, w/o) containing **more than 10% of water.** Pastes – semisolid dispersion system, where a **solid particles (> 25%, e.g. ZnO)** are dispersed in ointments – mostly oleaginous (Petrolatum).

Antioxidants which act by providing electrons and easily available hydrogen atoms that acceptable more readily by the **free radicals** (atoms containing one or more unpaired electrons as molecular oxygen O-O or free hydroxyl group (OH)

Examples of Antioxidants: Na2SO3, NaHSO3, H3PO2 and Ascorbic

In oligeanous preparation –

- ✓ Alpha tocopherol,
- ✓ BHA (butylhydroxyanisole),
- ✓ BHT (butyl hydroxytoluene)
- ✓ Ascorbic palmitate.

<u>**EXAMPLES:**</u>

Epinephrine preparations - Adrenergic - do not use the if it is brown or contains precipitate **Nitroglycerin Tablets** - Antianginal - to prevent loss of potency, keep these tablets in the original container

Paraldehyde - Hypnotic - subject to oxidation to form acetic acid.

<u>**POLYMORPHISM:**</u>

Important factor on formulation is the crystal or amorphous from of the drug substance.

The amorphous form of a compound is always **more soluble** than a corresponding **crystal form.**

The most widely used methods are hot stage microscopy, thermal analysis, **infrared spectroscopy, and x-ray diffraction.**

<u>**PROBABLE MODES OF ACTION OF SOME PRESERVATIVES**</u>

1. **Benzoic acid, boric acid, p-hydroxybenzoates:** Denaturation of proteins.
2. **Phenols, chlorinated phenolic cmpds:** lytic, denaturation action on cytoplasmic membranes and for chlorinated preservatives, also by oxidation of enzymes.

3. **Alcohols:** lytic and denaturation action on membranes. Quaternary compounds: Lytic action on membranes.

4. **Mercurials:** Denaturation of enzymes by combining with **thiol (-SH) groups.**

Flavoring Agents

*** To mask effectively the unwanted or disagreeable taste of drugs

In general, **low molecular weight are salty, like NaCl, KCl, NH4Cl, NaBr** and higher molecular salts are **bitter** except some lead salts.

Examples: Anise oil, Cinnamon, Peppermint, and Orange.

With organic compounds, an increase in the number of OH group seems to increase the sweetness of the compound. **Sucrose** which has **8 OH groups** is sweeter than **glycerin** which has **3 OH groups.**

SWEETENING PHARMACEUTICALS

SACCHARIN = metabolized and excreted by the kidneys virtually unchanged.

CYCLAMATE = metabolized or processed in digestive tract and it's by product are excreted by the kidneys.

ASPARTAME = breaks down in the body into three basic components: the amino acids **phenylalanine and aspartic acid, and methanol.**

Because of its metabolism to phenylalanine, the use of aspartame by persons with phenylketonuria (PKU) is discourages, and diet foods and drinks must bear appropriate label warning.

Saccharin and cyclamate were "Generally Recognized as Safe" or what is known as **GRAS.**

ACESULFAME = is more stable than aspartame at elevated temperature; It is use in candy, chewing gum, confectionery, and instant coffees and teas.

STEVIA POWDER = Stevia *Rebaudiana bertoni*.

It is natural, nontoxic, safe, and about **30 times** as sweet as cane sugar, or sucrose.

AESTHETIC VALUE

Liquid preparations - the amount is ranging from **0.0005 to 0.001%** depending upon the colorant and intensity desired_**Solid or powdered,**

Compressed Tablets - generally larger proportion is required **(0.1%**

Ointments, suppositories, opthalmic and parenteral -no color additives)

DISSOLUTION APPRATUS IP AND USP

APPRATUS	IP	USP
Apparatus 1	Paddle (37°)	Basket (37°)
Apparatus 2	Basket (37°)	Paddle (37°)
Apparatus 3	Reciprocating Cylinder (37°)	Reciprocating Cylinder (37°)
Apparatus 4	Flow-Through Cell (37 °)	Flow-Through Cell (37 °)
Apparatus 5	Paddle over Disk (32°)	Paddle over Disk (32°)
Apparatus 6	Cylinder (32°)	Cylinder (32°)
Apparatus 7	Reciprocating Holder	Reciprocating Holder

Some IMP Drug Interactions

S.N	DRUG INTERACTION	EFFECT
1	Aluminium Hydroxide Gel	Decrease effect of that drug due to increases pH of gastric fluid
2	Ciprofloxacin + Theophyline	Increases plasma level of Theophyline
3	Aminoglycoside + beta-Lactam antibiotics	synergestic effect but if given in same syring it's become inactive due to complex formation
4	Cortisone + Ampicillin	Antagonist
5	Erythromycin Telrithromycin Phenytoin +Clarithromycin/ Carmazepam/	Increases level of Phenytoin and Carbamazapine
6	Methotrexate + Sulfamethoxazole	Displace from binding site and increases free plasma concentration of drug

7	Amphotericin B + Flucytosine	Synergestic effect
8	Ketoconazole + Amphotericin B	Antagonized effect Due to ergosterol level decreases
9	Azoles (including All) + Terbinafine	Contraindicated
10	Posconazole + Ergot alkaloid	Contraindicate
11	Cimetidine + Terbinafine	Increases plasma Concentration of Terbinafine
12	Gresiofulvin + Alcohol	Potentiate toxicity of alcohol
13	Miconazole+ Warfarin	inhibit metabolism of warfarin
14	MAO inhibitors + Pethidine	Hyperpyrexia
15	TCA + SSRIs	TCA toxicity

GOLD NUMBER & PROTECTION OF COLLOIDS

• Lyophilic sols are more stable than lyophobic sols.

• Lyophobic sols can be easily coagulated by the addition of small quantity of an electrolyte.

• When a lyophilic sol is added to any lyophobic sol, it becomes less sensitive towards electrolytes. Thus, lyophilic colloids can prevent the coagulation of any lyophobic sol.

"The phenomenon of preventing the coagulation of a lyophobic sol due to the addition of some lyophilic colloid is called sol protection or protection of colloids."

•   The protecting power of different protective (lyophilic) colloids is different. The efficiency of any protective colloid is expressed in terms of gold number.

<u>**GOLD NUMBER**</u>

Zsigmondy introduced a term called gold number to describe the protective power of different colloids.

This is defined as, "weight of the dried protective agent in milligrams, which when added to 10 ml of a standard gold sol (0.0053 to 0.0058%) is just sufficient to prevent a colour change from red to blue on the addition of 1 ml of 10 % sodium chloride solution, is equal to the gold number of that protective colloid."

Thus, smaller is the gold number, higher is the protective action of the protective agent.

Protective power $\propto$ 1/Gold number

HYDROPHILIC SUBSTANCE	GOLD NUMBER
Gelatin	0.005 - 0.01
Sodium oleate	0.4 – 1.0
Sodium caseinate	0.01
Gum tragacanth	2
Hamoglobin	0.03 – 0.07
Potato starch	25
Gum arabic	0.15 – 0.25

1935	RBI established
1949	RBI Nationalized
2005	RTI ACT
2005	Product Patent In India
1956	Companies Act
1932	Partnership Act
1993	End of GATT era
1997	National Pharmaceutical Pricing Authority (NPPA)
1994	Dolly sheep – First clone
1950	First Planning Commission

1984	Hatch-Waxman Act
1955	SBI nationalized

2005	IPC constituted
1896	First Olympics
2000 (26 Jan.)	Human Genome Revealed
1970	Indian Patents Act
1919	Poison Act
1948	Pharmacy Act
1940	Drug and Cosmetic Act
1930	Dangerous Drug Act
1857	Opium Act
1954	Drug and Magic Remedies Act
1971	Medical Termination of Pregnancy Act (MTP)
1989	First ICH Indian pharmacopoeias:
1955	1st Edition IP
1966	2nd Edition IP
1985	3rd Edition IP
1996	4th Edition IP
2007	5th Edition IP
2010	6th Edition IP
2014	7th Edition IP

LIST OF WELL KNOWN POISONS & ANTIDOTES

POISONING	ANTIDOTE USED
Paracetamol	N-acetylcysteine
Anticoagulants (warfarin)	Vitamin K
Opioids	Naloxone
Iron (&other heavy metals)	Desferrioxamine, Deferasirox or Deferiprone
Benzodiazepines	Flumazenil
Ethylene glycol	Ethanol or fomepizole, and thiamine, methanol-

	ethanol or fomepizole, and folinic acid
Cyanide	Amyl nitrite, Sodium nitrite and Sodium thiosulfate
Organophosphates	Atropine and Pralidoxime
Magnesium	Calcium Gluconate
Ca++ Cha. Blockers Vera, Dilti. CCB	Calcium Gluconate
Beta-Blockers (Propranolol, Sotalol)	Calcium Gluconate and/or Glucagon
Isoniazid	Pyridoxine
Atropine	Physostigmine
Thallium	Prussian blue
Hydrofluoric acid	Calcium Gluconate
Anticholinergics	Cholinergics (&vice-versa)

SOME IMPORTANT FACTS GPAT NOTES

1. Lipid insoluble and water insoluble drugs are not absorbed from gut.
2. Most of the drugs are weakly acidic are weakly basic because stronger forms has high ability to form corresponding ions.
3. Most (90%) of drugs absorbed through passive diffusion(non-ionic diffusion)
4. 0% protein binding – Lisinopril
5. 99% protein binding - oxyphenbutazone (metabolite of phenylbutazone)
6. To show an efficient drug action protien binding should be moderate, insufficient protein binding shows less Vd & high protein binding lessens amount of drug at active site.
7. Extent of binding --------------albumin > acid glycoprotein > lipoprotein > globulins.
8. Drug having less Vd means its not bioavailable.(i.e decresed rate & amount of drug)
9. Bioavailability of Higher to Lower---------------parenteral > oral > rectal >

topical.

10. Short acting barbiturates are due its rapid rate of distribution from brain.

11. Only unbounded drug (free form) undergoes metabolism.

12. The unbound drug 1st reaches liver from where it goes to other parts like kidneys

13. Only lipid soluble and non-ionic drugs can enters brain.

14. All orally administerd drugs undergo first pass metabolism.

15. Propanolol & Ca++ channel blockers have extensive first pass metabolism.

16. Mainly metabolism occurs to excrete the drug.

17. Acidic drugs are exerted at basic pH & vice-versa.

18. Absorption, Distribution, Elimination follows 1st order kinetics.

19. Drugs showing 0 order elimination kinetics are asprin, ethanol, phenytoin, Theophyline, Tolbutamide, phenylbutazone, Warfarin, Heparin, salicylates etc.

20. Metabolism, Protein binding, carrier mediated transport at saturated conditions,

    IV infusion IM implants, osmatic pumps undergo 0 order kinetics i.e rate or process directly proportional to concentration or amount of reactants.

COUNTRY – CAPITAL – CURRENCY IMP FOR GPAT & NIPER JEE EXAM COUNTRY – CAPITAL – CURRENCY

1. France – Paris – France
2. Germany – Berlin – Deutsche Mar
3. Greece – Athens – Drachma
4. Hong Kong - Victoria – Dollar
5. India - New Delhi – Rupee
6. Indonesia - Jakarta – Rupiah
7. Iran - Teheran – Rial
8. Iraq - Baghdad – Dinar
9. Ireland – Dublin – Pound
10. Italy - Rome – Lira
11. Japan – Tokyo – Yen

12. Kenya - Nairobi – Shilling

13. Malaysia - Kuala Lumpur – Ringgit

14. Nepal – Kathmandu – Rupee

15. New Zealand - Wellington – Dollar

16. Oman - Muscat – Rial

17. Pakistan – Islamabad – Rupee

18. Qatar – Doha – Riyal

19. Russia - Moscow – Ruble

20. Saudi Arabia – Riyadh – Rial

21. Singapore – Singapore City – Dollar

22. South Africa - Madrid – Rand

23. Spain – Madrid – Peseta

24. Sri Lanka - Colombo – Rupee

25. Sweden - Stockholm – Krona

26. Switzerland – Berne – France

27. Russia – Moscow – Ruble

28. Ukraine – Kiev – Hyrvnia

29. Azerbaijan – Baku – Ruble

30. Thailand – Bangkok – Baht

31. United Arab Emirates (UAE) – Abu Dhabi – Dirham

32. United Kingdom (UK)-London – Pound Sterling

33. United States of America (US) -Washington – Dollar

34. Yemen – Sana – Rial

35. Zimbabwe -Harare – Dollar

DRUGS BANNED IN INDIA

➢ Tetracycline liquid oral suspension

➢ Penicillin skin/eye ointement

➢ Methaquinone

➢ Oxytetracycline liquid oral preperations

➢ Demeclocycline liquid oral preperations

➢ Rosiglitazone

➢ Astemizole

➢ Terfinadine

DIFFERENT TESTS FOR CARBOHYDRATE

Name of test	Use
Molisch test	Reducing sugars
Iodine test	Starches
Benedicts reagent test	Reducing sugars
Barfords Test	Same like Molisch test but reduction carried in mild acidic medium .to distinguish monosaccharide from disaccharides. - reducing sugars.
Seliwanoffs Test	Ketohexoses
Foulgers Test	Ketohexoses
Rapid furfural test	Ketohexoses
Osazone Test	-
Sucrose hydrolysis test	Sucrose

DIFFERENT TESTS FOR AMINO ACIDS AND PROTEINS

NAME OF TEST	USE
Biuret reaction	Two peptide linkage
Ninhydrin reaction	Alfa amino acids
Xanthoproteic reaction	Aromatic amino acids like, Phenylalanine, tyrosine, tryptophan
Milons reaction	Phenolic amino acids (tyrosine)
Hopkins kole reaction	Indole ring (tryptophan)
Sakaguchi reaction	Guanidino group (arginine)
Nitroprusside reaction	Sulfahydryl group (cysteine)
Sulfer test	Sulfahydryl group (cysteine)
Pauly's test	Imidazole ring (histidine)
Folin coicateau's test	Phenolic group (tyrosine)

DIFFERENT TESTS FOR BIOCHEMICAL CONSTITUENTS OF BODY

NAME OF TEST	USE/ DETECTION
Sodium hypobromide test	Urea
Specific urease test	Urea
Benedicts uric acid test	Uric acid
Mureoxide test	Uric acid (caffine, Theophyline etc.)
Jaffe's test	Creatinine
Benzatidine test	Blood in urine etc.
Rothera test	Ketone bodies
Hay's rest	Bile salt
Petterkofer's test	Bile salt
Gmelin test	Bile pigments
Fouchets test	Bile pigments

Folin wu method	Blood glucose estimation
O-toulidine method	Blood glucose estimation
Glucose –oxidase peroxidase (GOD-POD)	Blood glucose estimation
Van den Bergh reaction	Serum bilirubin
Henry-Caraways method	Serum uric acid
Western blot TEST	confirmatory test for AIDS

MECHANISM OF ACTION

1- DNA Dependent RNA Polymerase- Rifampcin

2- RNA Dependent DNA Polymerase- Zidovudine

3- Protein Synthesis Blocker- Erythromycin, Chloramphenicol & Tetracycline

4- ACE Inhibitor- Captopril

5- Ca Channel Blocker- Nifedipine, Diltiazem

6- COX Inhibitor- Asprin

7- GABA Facilitator- Benzodiazepines

8- Antimetabolites- Methotrexate

9- Loop Diuretics- Frusemide

10- High Ceiling Diuretics- Spironolactone

11- Alteration of bacterial DNA- Choloroquine

12- Inhibition of Viral replication- Amantidine, Acyclovir

13- H1 blocking agent- Mepyramine, Loratadine

14- H2 Blocking agent- Rantidine, Cimetidine, Famotidine, Cyprohaptidine

15- Proton Pump inhibitor- Omeprazole, ALL PRAZOLE

16- DNA Metabolism Inhibitors- Quinacrine (Mepacrine)

17- Spindle Poison Vinca, Griesofulvin

18- Folic acid synthesis inhibitor- DDS

19- GABA Inhibitor- Sodium Valproate

20- DNA Synthesis Prevention – Nalidixic Acid

21- Prostaglandin Synthesis Inhibition- Oxyphenbutazone, Ibuprofen

22- Mycolic acid synthesis inhibition- INH

23- Folic acid antagonist- MTX, PAS, DDS & Primethamine

24- Desruption of DNA structure- MNZ

25- Inhibition of cell wall synthesis- Beta lactam antibiotics (Penicillin)

26- Release of nor epinephrine- Ephedrine

27- Ergosterol Biosnythesis Inhibitors- Clotrimazole, Miconalzole, Ketoconazole

28- Ach esterase inhibitors- Physostigmine, Neostigmine, Edrophonium, Metrifonate

29- Reverse Transcriptase Inhibitors- Stavudine, zidovudine

30- Inhibition of HIV Protease- Amepranavir

31- DNA Gyrase Inhibitor- Cinoxacin

32- Inhibition of DNA Polymerase-Gossypol

33- NMDA Receptor Antagonist-Amantadine, Ketamine, Dextromethorphan, Memantine & Nitrous Oxide

34- DNA intercalating agent- Daunorubicin, Doxorubicin, Ellipticin & Ethidium

Bromide 35-Antim mitotic agent- Amphethenile

36-Alkylating agent- Thiotepa

37-Alpha receptor antagonist- Phentolamine

38-Beta receptor antagonist- Propanolol, Aplrenolol

39-Alpha receptor agonist-Norepinehrine

40-Beta receptor agonist- Isoproterenol & Salbutamol

41-DNA Adduct Formation- Procarbazine

42-Carbonic anhydrase inhibitor- Acetazolamide

43-Phosphodiestrase Inhibitor- Theophylline

44-Thrombin action prevention- Heparin

45-Xanthine oxidase inhibitor- Allopurinol

46-Cholinergic Blockade- Ipratropium

47-Adenosine Deaminase inhibitor- Crisnatapase

48-Immunomodulation- Imiquimod

49-Amino acid transfer interference- Econazole

50- Mast Cell Stabilization- Ketosifen

<u>DRUG & THEIR IMORTANT SIDE EFFECT</u>

1. Grey Baby Syndrome- Chloramphenicol

2. Pin Point Pupil, Straubb's syndrome-Morphine

3. Reyes Syndrome- Asprin

4. Urine Coloration- Rifampcin

5. Frontal Headache- Indomethacin

6. Captopril- Persistant dry cough

7. Bleomycin-Pulmonary fibrosis

8. Vancomycin- Red man syndrome

9. Nicotinic acid- Flush

10. Steven Johnsons syndrome- Allopurinol, Sulphonamides, Itraconazole

11. sulphonamides-kernicterus

12. aminoglycosides-ototoxicity

13. Discolouration of teeth-tetracyclines

14. Doxorubucin & duanorubucin- cardiomyopathy.

15. Chloroquine- Cardiotixicity, retinopathy, discolouration of hair

16. Doxycycline- esophageal ulceration

17. Vincristin & Vinblastin- Neuropathy

18. Cyclophosphamide- Alopecia, Pancretitis

19. Cimetidine & Spironolactone - Gynaecomastia

20. Jaurisch hexheimer reaction- Penicillin

21. Blue baby syndrome- Amiodarone

22. Nephrotoxicity- Cisplatin

23. Shake and bake syndrome-Amphotericin B

24. S-Thallidomide-Phocomelia

25. Phenytoin-Gingival hyperplasia

26. Valproic acid-curling of hair

27. Carbamazepine- Aplastic anaemia

28. Anticholinergics- Atropine fever

MICROSCOPY OF SOME IMPOTANT DRUGS

1- Liquorice- Ulignified Septate fibre

2- Solanacoeus Plants- Anisocytic stomata

3- Rhubarb- Star spots

4- Squill- Ca oxide raphides

5- Cardamom- Clothing of glandular trichome

6- Quillaria- Thin membrane arillus

7- Digitalis- Rhytidomes & Glandular Trichomes

8- Atropa Belladona- Anisocytic Stomata

9- Verbascus Thapsus- Clusters of Ca Oxalate

10-   Artemisia- T-Shaped Trichomes

11-   Stromanium- Phloem Fibres

12-   Nuxvomica – Lignified trichomes

13-   Fennel- Reticulate lignified trichomes

14-   Coriander- Wavy sclerenchyma

15-   Indian Dill- Lateral ridges with vascular bundle

16-   Anise- Branched & unbranched vittae

17-		Cinnamon- Absence of cork & cortex

18-		Ginger- Non Lignified vessels & starch grains, Endodermis with no starch

19-		Collapsed Endodermis

20-		Caraway-Collapsed Parenchyma

21-		Chenopodium-Epidermis with no trichomes

22-		Chirata- Stomata on lower surface only with no trichomes

23-		Cinchona - Large sclerenchymatous bast cells with medullary ray.

24-		Cinnamon- Parenchyma cells with starch.

25-		Colchicum- Spiral Ducts, Parenchyma with starch

26-		Coriander- Prismatic and aggregate crystals of calcium oxalate

27-		Saffron- Trichome of stigma

28-		Turmeric- Parenchyma with pasty starch

29-		Digitalis- Glandular trichomes

30-		Euclyptus- Crystal bearing fiber

31-		Gentian- Large reticulate ducts

32-		Liquorice- Parenchyma with crystals and starch

33-		Hycyamus- Endosperm tissue with proteid granules and oil.

34-		Ipecac- Parenchyma with raphides

35-		Mentha- Trichomes, simple, showing cuticular markings (a medium sized trichome).

36-		Pilocarpus- Aggregate crystals of calcium oxalate.

37-		Podophyllum- Reticulate ducts and tracheids, Spiral duct, Aggregate crystals of calcium oxalate, Cork

38-		Quassia- Medullary ray with starch, large porous duct

39-		Rheum- Parenchyma with starch, resin and crystals, reticulate ducts.

40-		Senega- Parenchyma with fat, Cork & Porous duct.

41-		Senna- Bast of vascular bundles, Crystal bearing fibers from vascular tissue

42-		Stromanium- Parenchyma cells of petiole

43-		Strophanthus- Endosperm tissue, showing oil and crystals, Outer tissue with granular proteid matter and starch

44-   Tobbaco- Parenchyma (collenchymatous) from midrib, Leaf parenchyma with chlorophyll.

45-   Ginger- Parenchyma with starch and one cell with resin

46-   Belladona- Tracheids and spiral duct, Leaf parenchyma cells with crystals, Bast Cells, Porous ducts & Crystal Sand

DRUG OF CHOISE IMP FOR GPAT

1. Paracetamol poisoning - acetyl cysteine

2. Acute bronchial asthma – salbutamol

3. Acute gout – NSAIDS

4. Acute Hyperkalemia - calcium gluconate

5. Severe DIGITALIS toxicity – DIGIBIND

6. Acute migraine – sumatriptan

7. Cheese reaction – Phentolamine

8. Atropine poisoning – physostigmine

9. Cyanide poisoning - Amyl nitrite

10. Benzodiazepine poisoning – flumazenil

11. Cholera – tetracycline

12. KALA-AZAR - Lipozomal amphotericin- B

13. Iron poisoning – Desferrioxamine

14. MRSA - vancomycin

15. VRSA – LINEZOLID

16. Warfarin Overdose - vitamin-K

17. OCD – fluoxetine

18. Alcohol Poisoning – fomepizole

19. Epilepsy in pregnency – Phenobarbitone

20. Anaphylactic shock - Adrenaline

<u>**CANIZZARO REACTION**</u>

THE ALDEHIDE DO NO HAVE ALFA HIDROGEN GIVES CANIZARO REACTION IN PRESENCE OF CONCE. NaOH

2 Molecule of Aldehide + conc. NaOH => ALCOHOL + CARBOXILIC ACID

ONE MOLECULE OF ALDEHIDE GET REDCTION REACTION & PRODUCE ALCOHOL, OTHER GOT OXIDATION PRODUCE CARBOXILIC ACID

<u>**SOME IMPORTANT TOPICS FOR GPAT FROM TABLET AND CAPSULE**</u>

➢ <u>**PICKING AND STICKING**</u>

This is when the coating removes a piece of the tablet from the core. Overwetting or examples or excessive film tackiness causes tablets to stick to each other or to the coating pan. On drying, at the point of contact, a piece of the film may remain adhered to the pan or to another tablet, giving a **"picked"** appearance to the tablet surface and resulting in a small exposed area of the core. It is caused by over-wetting the tablets, by under-drying, or by poor tablet quality.

REMEDY: <u>A reduction in the liquid application rate or increase in the drying air temperature and air volume usually solves this problem. Excessive tackiness may be an indication of a poor formulation.</u>

➢ <u>**TWINNING**</u>

<u>This is the term for two tablets that stick together, and it's a common problem with capsule shaped tablets.</u>

REMEDY - Assuming you don't wish to change the tablet shape, you can solve this problem by balancing the pan speed and spray rate. Try reducing the spray rate or increasing the pan speed. In some cases, it is necessary to modify the design of the tooling by very slightly changing the radius. The change is almost impossible to see, but it prevents the twinning problem.

➢ <u>**COLOR VARIATION**</u>

This problem can be caused by processing conditions or the formulation. Improper mixing, uneven spray pattern and insufficient coating may result in color variation. The migration of soluble dyes, plasticizers and other additives during drying may give the coating a mottled or spotted appearance.

REMEDY:

1. The use of lake dyes eliminates dye migration.
2. A reformulation with different plasticizers and additives is the best way to solve film instabilities caused by the ingredients.

➤ **ORANGE PEEL EFFECT**

This refers to a coating texture that resembles the surface of an orange. Inadequate spreading of the coating solution before drying causes a bumpy or "orange-peel" effect on the coating. It is usually the result of high atomization pressure in combination with spray rates that are too high. This also indicates that spreading is impeded by too rapid drying or by high solution viscosity.

REMEDY: Thinning the solution with additional solvent may correct this problem.

➤ **MOTTLED COLOR**

This can happen when the coating solution is improperly prepared, the actual *spray rate differs from the target rate*, the tablet cores are cold, or the drying rate is out of specification.

➤ **CAPPING AND LAMINATION**

This is when the tablet separates in laminar fashion. Capping is partial or complete separation of top or bottom crowns of tablet main body. Lamination is separation of a tablet into two or more distinct layers. Friability test can be used to reveal these problems

The problem stems from improper tablet compression, but it may not reveal itself until you start coating. How you operate the coating system, however, can exacerbate the problem.

REMEDY: Be careful not to over-dry the tablets in the preheating stage. That can make the tablets brittle and promote capping.

➤ **ROUGHNESS**

 Some of the droplets may dry too rapidly before reaching the tablet bed, resulting in the deposits on the tablet surface of "spray dried" particles instead of finely divided droplets of coating solution. Surface roughness also increases with pigment concentration and polymer concentration in the coating solution.

REMEDY: Moving the nozzle closer to the tablet bed and reducing the degree of atomization can decrease the roughness due to "spray drying".

HAZING / DULL FILM

This is sometimes called Bloom. It can occur when too high a processing temperature is used for a particular formulation. Dulling is particularly evident when cellulosic polymers are applied out of aqueous media at high processing temperatures. It can also occur if the coated tablets are exposed to high humidity conditions and partial salvation of film results.

➢ BRIDGING

This occurs when the coating fills in the lettering or logo on the tablet and is typically caused by improper application of the solution, poor design of the tablet embossing, high coating viscosity, high percentage of solids in the solution, or improper atomization pressure. During drying, the film may shrink and pull away from the sharp corners of an intagliation or bisect, resulting in a "bridging" of the surface. This defect can be so severe that the monogram or bisect is completely obscured.

REMEDY: Increasing the plasticizer content or changing the plasticizer can decrease the incidence of bridging.

➢ FILLING

Filling is caused by applying too much solution, resulting in a thick film that fills and narrows the monogram or bisect. In addition, if the solution is applied too fast, Overwetting may cause the liquid to quickly fill and be retained in the monogram.

REMEDY: Judicious monitoring of the fluid application rate and thorough mixing of the tablets in the pan can prevent filling.

- ➤ **EROSION** This can be the result of soft or friable tablets (and the pan turning too fast), an over-wetted tablet surface, inadequate drying, or lack of tablet surface strength.

- ➤ **PEELING AND FROSTING**

  This is a defect where the coating peels away from the tablet surface in a sheet. Peeling indicates that the coating solution did not lock into the tablet surface. This could be due to a defect in the coating solution, over-wetting, or high moisture content in the tablet core which prevented the coating to adhering.

  CHIPPING

  This is the result of high pan speed, a friable tablet core, or a coating solution that lacks a good plasticizer

- ➤ **BLISTERING**

  When coated tablets require further drying in ovens, too rapid evaporation of the solvent from the core and the effect of high temperature on the strength, elasticity and adhesion of the film may result in blistering.

  REMEDY: Milder drying conditions are warranted in this case.

- ➤ **CRACKING**

  It occurs if internal stresses in the film exceed the tensile strength of the film.

  REMEDY: tensile strength of the film can be increased by Using higher molecular weight polymers or polymer blends.

  TABLET AND CAPSULE MACHINES

  1. Rotosort- for filled/unfilled capsule sorting machine and for de-dusting.

  2. Rotofill- to fill pellets in hard gelatin capsule

  3. Rotoweigh- A high speed capsule weighing machine.

  4. Accogel- filling of dry powder in soft gelatin capsule. Accofill- fill exact powder dose in hard gelatin capsule

  5. Wurster- for coating.

  6. Osaka- capsule filling machine (powder, granules)

  7. Zanasi- capsule filling (powder, pellets, tablets)

  8. Lily/parke-davis: capsule filling (powder)

9. Farmatic, holfiger & kary-liquid filling in HGC.

10. Erweka- De-dusting and polishing capsule machine.

11. Seidender- Uses a Belt for visual inspection.

12. Vericap 1200- capsule weighing machine.

PHYTOCHEMICAL SCREENING OF DIFFERENT CLASSES OF DRUGS IN PHARMACOGNOSY NOTES FOR GPAT

Phytochemical screening is done to identify the nature and type of constituents present in a drug. This technique is of extreme help when a new drug is being investigated for the chemical constituents. In phytochemical screening there are both general and specific tests for finding the nature of chemical constituents in the drug. This topic is very simple and short but contains due weightage in the GPAT due to its importance in the pharmacognosy. Here I am discussing the topic in detail stressing on the regions important from the perspective of GPAT.

❖ **GENERAL CHEMICAL TESTS FOR ALKALOIDS:**

Alkaloids are tested by the following reagents. Each reagent or test has accuracy and specificity.

i) **Dragendroff's reagent-** This reagent is constituted of Potassium Bismuth Iodide (PBI). Alkaloids give reddish brown color with the dragendroff's reagent.

ii) **Mayer's reagent-** This reagent is constituted of Potassium Mercuric Iodide (PMI). Alkaloids give cream color with the Mayer's reagent. Remember M for Mayer M for Mercuric

iii) **Wagner's reagent-** This reagent is constituted of Iodine Potassium Iodide (IPI). Alkaloids give reddish brown precipitate with the Wagner's reagent.

iv) **Hager's reagent-** This reagent is constitutes of Picric Acid. Alkaloids give yellow precipitate with the Hager's reagent.

v) **Tannic acid-** With tannic acid alkaloids give buff colored precipitate.

vi) **Picrolinic acid-** Yellow colored precipitate are produced with picrolinic acid.

❖ **<u>CHEMICAL TESTS FOR GLYCOSIDES:</u>**

❖ **<u>General test for glycosides- The general test for glycoside is as follows-</u>**

Test A- Dissolve the 200 mg <u>drug with sulphuric acid</u>. Then, add <u>5% NaOH</u> solution for neutralization. Add Fehling solution A & B to the above mixture. <u>Red color</u> is produced.

Test B- Dissolve the 200 mg <u>drug with sufficient amount of water</u>. Add further water <u>to dilute</u> the solution. This solution is tested with <u>Fehling solution A & B</u>. Red color is produced from the reducing sugar present in the drug.

☐ Compare the red color from the two tests of the drug.

☐ If the color of test A is more intense than test B; glycoside presence confirmed. **<u>CHEMICAL TEST FOR ANTHRAQUINONE GLYCOSIDES-</u>**

Brontrager's test- This test is performed for the O-glycosides. Drug is dissolved in 1ml H2SO4 and mixture is boiled. Filter the solution, filterate is then mixed with chloroform. Chloroform layer mixed with ammonia gives rose pink color if O-glycosides are present.

Modified brontrager's test- This test is performed for the investigation of C-glycosides. Drug is mixed with H2SO4 and FeCl3. The next procedure is same as for the O-glycosides in brontrager's test.

Hydroxy anthraquinones- Drug is mixed with Potassium Hydroxide. If hydroxy anthraquinones are present red color is present.

❖ **<u>CHEMICAL TEST FOR CARDIAC GLYCOSIDES-</u>**

Kedde's test- Extract the drug with CHCl3. 90% alcohol with 2% 3, 5-dinitrobenzoic acid is added to the extract. To this mixture 20% NaOH is added. Purple color confirms the presence of cardiac glycoside.

Keller-killiani test- This test is performed only for the digitoxose sugar moiety. Drug is extracted with chloroform first. 0.4 ml acetic acid is added then along with FeCl3. After adding H2SO4 if purple color is produced in the acid layer then presence of digitoxose sugar confirmed.

Raymond's test- Reagent used in this test is Methanolic alkali. Violet color confirms the presence of cardiac glycosides.

Legal's test- This test is performed by using pyridine and alkaline sodium nitroprusside is used. Red color is produced if cardiac glycoside is present.

Baljet test- Reagent used in this test is picric acid and sodium picrate. Orange color is produced in the presence of cardiac glycoside.

❖ **CHEMICAL TEST OF CYANOGENETIC GLYCOSIDE-**

Sodium picrate test- Drug is mixed with dilute H_2SO_4. After the addition of sodium picrate red color is produced in the presence of cyanogenetic glycoside.

Mercuric acetate test- After mixing the mercuric acetate with drug. Drug acetate is formed and mercury is separated out which confirms the presence of cyanogenetic glycoside.

❖ **CHEMICAL TEST FOR STEROIDS & TERPENOIDS:**

i)   **Liberman-Burchard test-** Drug is mixed with acetic anhydride. To this mixture con. Sulfuric acid is added. There forms two layers with browning at the junction. Upper layer with green color represents steroids whereas lower layer represents terpenoids red color.

ii)   **Salwoski test-** Drug is mixed with con. Sulfuric acid. Upper layer is of steroids which are red in color and lower yellow colored layer represents trirepenes.

iii)   **Sulphur powder test-** If sulfur is added to the mixture of drug, sulfur sinks down the mixture.

❖ **CHEMICAL TEST FOR FLAVONOIDS:**

i)   **Shinoda test-** Shinoda test is performed by adding magnesium along with the HCl in the drug mixture. Red/pink/green to blue color confirms the presence of flavonoids.

ii)   Alkaline reagent test- As the name suggests, an alkaline reagent is used for this test. Sodium hydroxide is added to the drug. Yellow color is produced; if on addition of dilute acid this color disappears then it confirms the presence of flavonoids.

iii) ZnHCl test- Flavonoids give red color with the Zinc hydrochloride.

❖ **E) CHEMICAL TESTS FOR TANNINS:**

i)   Gold beater's skin test- This is most common test for tannins. This test is performed on the membrane of OX. Goldbeater's skin is first treated with HCl and rinsed with distilled water. After this, this skin is paced in the solution of drug and rinsed with water. After addition of 1% $FeSO_4$, brown or black color is produced in the skin due to the presence of tannins.

ii) FeCl3 test- Yellow color is produced with FeCl3 in the case of hydrolysable tannins whereas condensed tannins give green color.

iii) Phenazone test- Sodium phosphate is mixed with drug and filtered. To the filtrate phenazone is added which produce precipitate if tannins are present.

iv) Gelatin test- Precipitate is produced with gelatin which confirms the presence of tannins.

F) CHEMICAL TESTS FOR VOLATILE OILS:

i) Volatile containing drugs when mixed with alcoholic solution of Sudan III gives red color.

ii) Volatile oil containing crude drugs also produces red color with tincture alkane.

<u>**TABLET DOSAGE FORM**</u>

Tablet is the most common solid dosage forms prescribed and accepted worldwide. Although there are various types of tablets available in the market depending upon the size, use and formulation but the basic excipients used in the formulation of tablet are same everywhere.

❖ <u>**What is tablet?**</u>

In simple language, tablet is a solid dosage from comprised of active pharmaceutical ingredient along with several excipients for attaining the desirable biological and pharmaceutical properties. From an estimate, two-third of the prescribed medicines in the world is tablet. Most of the tablets are given through oral route but depending on the need and patient's concition it can also be given rectally, vaginally, buccally and sub-lingually.

Size and shape of the tablet also vary according to the formulation and need of the patient. Some tablets are just of few millimeters while other go up to 1 centimeter. Also, shape of the tablet can also be either oval, round, capsule shaped etc.

Formulation of the tablet: Different excipients used in the tablet

Beside from the active ingredient, tablet contains various other ingredients like diluents, binder, disintegrant, glidant and lubricant. Chief role of the excilients in the tablet formulation is to impart desirable pharmaceutical and biological properties to the tablet. Here is the detail of the different excipients used in the formulation of the tablet.

➢ <u>**DILUENT**</u>

The main role of the diluents in the tablet formulation is to impart bulk to the tablet. Generally, the active ingredient required in a single tablet ranges from 1 mg to 1000 mg. So, it is not possible to make a tablet with such small weight therefore diluent is mixed with the active compound. Major diluents used in the tablet formulation include-

a) CaCO3- Insoluble in water

b) α-Lactose- Most common, inexpensive and inert

c) Mannitol- Used for chewable tablets

d) Microcrystalline cellulose- Increase disintegrant property also

> **DISINTEGRANTS**

Disintegrants are used for the purpose of breaking the tablet when introduced in the biological system. Mainly water and pH of the system are responsible for the disintegration of the tablet. Tablet after disintegration releases its active constituent into the system which exerts its pharmacological action. Disintegrants used in the tablet are-

a) Alginic acid/Na Alginate – Used concentration is 2-10% w/v

b) Na carboxy methyl cellulose (Nymcel) - Used concentration is 1-20% w/v

c) Microcrystalline cellulose (Avicel) - Used concentration is 10% w/v

d) Starch - Used concentration is 2-10% w/v

> **BINDERS (GRANULATING AGENT)**

Binders are used to increase the cohesive forces between the ingredients of the tablet so that tablet can be compressed easily. The concentration of the binder should be used carefully as it can greatly influence the properties of the tablet. Binders used in the tablet formulation are:

a) Acacia mucilage (20%) - It gives very hard granules.

b) Gelatin (5-20%)

c) PVP (2-10%) – Used for Non-aqueous granulation

d) Starch (5-10%) - Common binder

e) Tragacanth (20%) – Gives hard granules

> **GLIDANTS/FILLER**

Glidants are used to enhance the flow properties of the granules or powders so that granules do not stick with each other. Mainly at present there are only two types of glidants used in the tablet formulation:

a) Colloidal Silica (0.1-0.5%) – Most common and excellent glidant properties

b) Talc (1-2%)

> **LUBRICANTS**

Lubricants are used for the comfortable ejection of the tablet from punching machine without sticking to the die walls. Lubricants used in the tablet formulation include-

a) Stearic acid

b) Liquid Paraffin (5%)

c) Na Benzoate (5%)

d) Na Lauryl sulphate (0.5-5%)

(For tablet and capsule chapter LACHMAN is the best book for GPAT so also refer the LACHMAN once along with this study material)

MICROBIOLOGY

Reduction in numbers and / or activity of the total Achieved by

• Physical agents

• Chemical agents

• Chemotherapeutic agents

❖ **Antimicrobial action is influenced by some factors:**

• Environment: Effectiveness of heat is greater in presence of water, acid than in alkali, consistency of the material (aqueous or viscous), and presence of organic matter.

• Kinds of microorganisms: Growing vegetative cells more susceptible than spore forms, bacterial spores most resistant of all living organisms.

• Physiological state of cells: Young actively metabolizing cells more susceptible than old, dormant cells.

❖ **Mode of action of antimicrobial agents:**

• Damage to the cell wall or inhibition of cell wall synthesis

• Alteration of the permeability of the cytoplasmic membrane

• Alteration of the physical or chemical state of proteins and nucleic acids

• Inhibition of enzyme action

• Inhibition of protein or nucleic acid synthesis

❖ **Control by Physical agents:**

• High temperature

• Low temperature

•   Desication : Time of survival of microorganisms after desiccation depends upon factors – kind of microorganisms, material on which the organisms are dried, completeness of drying process, physical conditions to which the dried organisms are exposed – light, temperature, humidity..

• Osmotic pressure

•   Radiations – Ionising radiations: knock out electrons from molecules and ionize them forming hydrogen radicals, hydroxyl radicals, peroxides.

•   Non-ionising radiations: less energetic, absorbed specifically by different compounds causing excitation of their electrons and raise them to higher energy levels.

- UV radiations are absorbed most specifically by nucleic acids – pyrimidine dimers thus inhibiting DNA replication and resulting mutations.
- Filters – HEPA (high efficiency particulate air) filters.

Control by Chemical agents

General terms for use with various chemical agents of control:

- Sterilization: is a process in which all viable life forms are either killed or removed.
- Disinfectant: kills growing forms not necessarily the spores of disease producing organisms
- Disinfection: Process of killing infectious agents
- Antiseptic: that opposes sepsis. Usually associated with substances applied to the body
- Sanitizer: that reduces the microbial population to safe levels. Applied to equipment and utensils used in food industries, restaurants etc.
- Germicide (microbicide): that kills vegetative forms but not necessarily the spores of germs/microorganisms.
- Bactericide: that kills bacteria
- Bacteriostatic: A condition in which the growth of bacteria is prevented.
- Chemotherapeutic agents: used to treat infections.

Major groups of chemical antimicrobial agents:

Phenols and phenolic compounds:

Phenol was the first disinfectant used in 1880 by Joseph Lister to reduce the infection of surgical incisions. Used as a standard against which other disinfectants are compared to determine their antimicrobial activity. Cresol, phenyl phenol etc. are very effective disinfectants. A 5% solution of phenol rapidly kills the vegetative cells of microorganisms.

- **Mode of action:**

Precipitation of proteins, inactivation of enzymes, leakage of amino acids from cells.

Phenol coefficient technique: Test organisms are *Salmonella typhi* or *Staphylococcus aureus.* It is calculated by dividing the greatest dilution of the disinfectant killing the test organism in 10 min but not in 5 min with the greatest dilution of the phenol showing the same result.

Alcohols: Ethyl alcohol in concentrations between 50 and 90% is effective against vegetative or non-spore forming cells. Methyl alcohol is less bactericidal, higher alcohols – propyl, butyl, amyl are more germicidal than ethyl alcohol but since the alcohols higher than propyl are not miscible with water, they are not commonly used in disinfectants.

- **Mode of action:** Protein denaturants, also damage the lipid complex in cell membrane.

Halogens:

Iodine is one of the oldest and most effective germicidal agents.

Tincture of iodine. Also used in the form of substances – iodophores – Mixtures of iodine with surface-active agents – polyvinylpyrrolidone (PVP).

- **Mode of action:** Oxidises and inactivates essential metabolic compounds – Proteins with sulfhydryl groups.

- Chlorine and chlorine compounds: Chlorine gas, hypochlorites, chloramines.

- **Mode of action:** when chlorine is added in water it forms hypochlorous acid which is further decomposed to form nascent oxygen. Nascent oxygen being a strong oxidizing agent denatures major cellular constituents. Chlorine can also combine directly with proteins of cell membranes and enzymes.

$$Cl_2 + H_2O = HCl + HClO \text{ (hypochlorous acid)} \quad HClO = HCl + O$$

❖ **Heavy metals and their compounds:**

Mercury, silver, copper. By combining with cellular proteins especially containing sulfhydryl groups and inactivating them.

❖ **Dyes:**

• Triphenylmethane dyes - malachite green, brilliant green, crystal violet. Gram +ve bacteria more susceptible than gram –ve. Interfere with cellular oxidation processes.

• Acridine dyes – acriflavine, tryptoflavine. Selective inhibition against staphylococci and gonococci.

Synthetic detergents:

Detergents are wetting agents, surface tension depressants.

• **Anionic detergents** – those with detergent property resident in the anion Soap, Sodium lauryl sulphate (SLS).

• **Cationic detergents** – those with detergent property resident in cation Cetylpyridinium chloride. Cationic detergents are more germicidal than anionic compounds.

• **Quaternary ammonium compounds**: Most of germicidal cationic-detergent

☐ Compounds are quaternary ammonium salts in which R1, R2, R3 and R4 groups are

☐ Carbon groups linked to the nitrogen atom.

☐ The bactericidal power is high againt Gram+ve bacteria.

Mode of action: denaturation of proteins, interference with glycolysis and Membrane damage.

Aldehydes:

Most effective are formaldehyde and gluteraldehyde. Highly reactive chemicals – combine readily with vital nitrogen compounds – proteins, nucleic acids.

Gaseous agents:

Ethylene oxide – powerful sterilizing agent – liquid at <10.8oC – highly flammable.

• **Mode of action** – Alkylation reactions with organic compounds – enzymes and proteins.

Antibiotics and other chemotherapeutic agents:

• Inhibition of cell wall synthesis

• Damage to cytoplasmic membrane

• Inhibition of nucleic acid and protein synthesis

• Inhibition of specific enzyme systems

• **Inhibition of cell wall synthesis:** Penicillins, ampicillin, cephalosporins – interfere with final stages of Peptidoglycan synthesis – inhibit transpeptidase reaction – cross-linking of the two linear polymers. Cycloserine, vancomycin - inhibits the enzymes involved in the synthesis of pentapeptide side chains.

• **Damage to cytoplasmic membrane:** Polymyxins, Gramicidins, Tyrocidines – act on membrane having sterols – fungi and animal cells but not bacteria.

• **Inhibition of nucleic acid and protein synthesis:** Streptomycin, tetracycline – interfere with binding of 30S ribosomes, chloramphenicol, erythromycin - binds with 50s ribosome.

• **Inhibition of specific enzyme systems** – Sulfonamides

Antifungal antibiotics – Nystatin, Griseofulvin

Synthetic chemotherapeutic agents: Nitrofurans – both g+ve and g-ve bacteria,

Nalidixic acid – Inhibition of DNA synthesis in g-ve bacteria.

❖ **CONTROL OF MICROORGANISMS IN FOODS**

Aseptic handling

High Temperature – Boiling, Steam under pressure, Pasteurization, Sterilization,

Aseptic processing

Low Temperature – Refrigeration, Freezing,

Dehydration

Osmotic pressure – In concentrated sugar, brine

Chemicals – Organic acids, SO2, substances developing during food processing, substances contributed by microbial activity (acids)

Radiations – Ionizing radiations, non-ionizing radiations

High Temperature: One of the safest and most reliable methods. Steam under pressure cooker, most effective as it destroys all vegetative cells and spores.

Canning – $100^{O}C$ for high acid foods, $121^{O}C$ for low acid foods.

Pasteurization: LTH T– $145^{O}F$ ($62.8^{O}C$) for 30 min, HTST – $161^{O}F$ ($71.7^{O}C$) for 15 sec. This destroys all yeasts, Molds, gm-ve bacteria and most gram+ve bacteria.

Most heat resistant pathogen Coxiella Burnetti is also killed.

Sterilization: UHT -140-$150^{O}C$ for few seconds.

To understand thermal destruction of microorganisms for use in Food Preservation it is necessary to understand certain basic concepts:

Thermal Death Time (TDT): Time necessary to destroy a given population of microorganisms at a specified time.

Thermal Death Point (TDP): Temperature necessary to destroy a given population of microorganisms in a fixed time, usually 10 min.

Decimal reduction Time (D Value): Time necessary to destroy 90% of the organisms at a particular temperature.

Z Value: Temperature in ^{O}F required to vary D value by 90%.

D Value: Indicates resistance of microorganisms of to a specified temperature.

Z Value Indicates relative resistance to different temperatures.

Z value is used to construct equivalent thermal processes. At $220^{O}F$, D value = 113 min

At $203.5^{O}F$, D value = 1130 min (If Z value is 17.5 ^{O}F) At $237.5^{O}F$, D value = 11.3 min (If Z value is 17.5 ^{O}F)

<u>Aseptic Packaging:</u> In traditional canning methods non-sterile food is placed in a non-sterile metal/glass container followed by container closure and sterilization.

In aseptic packaging sterile food is placed in a sterile container under aseptic conditions and sealed under aseptic conditions.

Low temperature: Activities of spoilage organisms are lowered or stopped.

Dehydration: Drying reduces the a_w and thus prevents the growth of microorganisms. **Osmotic pressure:** NaCl and sugars exert drying effect – Plasmolysis – death.

Halodurics, halophiles, Osmophiles tolerate the high osmotic pressure.

Direct antimicrobials:

Benzoic acid and parabens:

C_6H_5COOH and its sodium salt –

$C_7H_5NaO_2$ along with esters of p-Hydroxybenzoic acid (Parabens).

Antimicrobial activity of benzoate is affected by pH – <u>Greatest activity at low pH – Ineffective at neutral pH.</u>

<u>ANTIMICROBIAL ACTIVITY RESIDES IN UN-DISSOCIATED MOLECULE</u>

☐ At pH 4.0 60% compound is un-dissociated.

☐ At pH 6.0 only 1.5% compound is un-dissociated.

Effective against yeasts and molds.

Generally employed in high acid foods – Apple juice, Soft drinks, Tomato ketchup and Salads.

Max permissible limit is 0.1%

Common permissible parabens are <u>heptyl-. Methyl-, propyl-, butyl-, ethyl-,</u>

Parabens less sensitive to pH than benzoate – effective upto pH 8.0

Both benzoate, and parabens block oxidation of glucose to pyruvic acid. Also inhibit uptake of substrate molecules.

<u>SORBIC ACID:</u>

$CH_3CH=CHCH+CHCOOH$ – usually employed as Ca, Na or K salt.

Permissible limit is 0.2%

Like benzoate also active in acid foods than neutral foods Generally in-effective at pH >6.5.

☐ At pH 4.0, 86% un-dissociated

☐ At pH 6.0, 6% compound is un-dissociated

Generally effective against molds and yeasts but also to certain bacteria. Generally used in bakery products, cheese, fruit juices, beverages, salad dressings. **Inhibits dehydrogenase enzyme system.**

Also inhibition of cellular uptake of substrate molecules – amino acids, phosphate, organic acids.

PROPIONIC ACID:

CH_3CH_2COOH as Ca and Na salts.

Mainly a mold inhibitor – used in breads, cakes, cheese. At pH 4.0 88% is un-dissociated

At pH 6.0 6.7% is un-dissociated

Inhibits cellular uptake of substrate molecules.

SULPHUR DIOXIDE AND SULPHITES:

SO_2, Na or K salts of SO_3 (sulphite), HSO_3 (Bisulphite), S_2O_5 (metabisulphite). Generally effective againt bacteria

Aerobes more sensitive than anaerobes More active at acidic pH

SO_2 < pH 3.0. HSO_3 at pH 3.0-5.0, SO_3 > pH 6.0.

At higher concentration yeasts and molds are also inhibited. Permissible limit is 100-200 ppm

Effect is due to reducing power – reduces the O_2 tension to a point at which aerobes are not able to grow. Also act on enzyme systems – enzyme poison – generally act on disulphide bonds.

Also used in dried foods to prevent enzymatic browning.

NITRITES AND NITRATES:

Many bacteria are capable of utilizing nitrate as electron acceptor which is reduced to nitrite highly reactive and capable of serving both reducing and oxidizing agent.

Under acidic conditions it ionizes to form nitrous acid (HONO) – further decomposes to give nitric oxide (NO) – capable of reacting with catalase, peroxidases, and cytochromes thus inhibiting aerobic bacteria.

1. What is Regulatory Affairs?

Ans-Regulatory Affairs in a Pharmaceutical industry, is a profession which acts as the interface between the pharmaceutical industry and Drug Regulatory authorities across the world. It is mainly involved in the registration of the drug products in respective countries prior to their marketing.

2. What are the goals of Regulatory Affairs Professionals?

Ans- Protection of human health Ensuring safety, efficacy and quality of drugs Ensuring appropriateness and accuracy of product information.

3. What are the Roles of Regulatory Affairs professionals?

Ans- Act as a liaison with regulatory agencies Preparation of organized and scientifically valid NDA, ANDA,INDA ,MAA,DMF submissions Ensure adherence and compliance with all the applicable cGMP, ICH, GCP, GLP guidelines, regulations and laws Providing expertise and regulatory intelligence in translating regulatory requirements into practical workable plans Advising the companies on regulatory aspects and climate that would affect their proposed activities Apart from the above main roles, there are various other roles which Regulatory Affairs professionals play.

4. What is an Investigational New Drug (IND) application?

Ans- It is an application which is filed with FDA to get approval for legally testing an experimental drug on human subjects in the USA

5. What is a New Drug Application?

Ans- the NDA is the vehicle through which drug sponsors formally propose that the FDA approve a new pharmaceutical for sale and marketing in the U.S. The data gathered during the animal studies and human clinical trials of an Investigational new drug become part of the NDA In simple words, "It is an application which is filed with FDA to market a new Pharmaceutical for sale in USA".

6. What is an Abbreviated New Drug Application (ANDA)?

Ans- It is an application filed with FDA, for a U.S. generic drug approval for an existing licensed medication or approved drug. In simple words, "It is an application for the approval of Generic Drugs ".

7. What is a Generic Drug Product?

Ans- A generic drug product is the one that is comparable to an innovator drug product in dosage form, strength, route of administration, quality, performance characteristics and intended use.

8. What is a DMF?

Ans- A Drug Master File (DMF) is a submission to the Food and Drug Administration (FDA) that may be used to provide confidential detailed information about facilities, processes, or articles used in the manufacturing, processing, packaging, and storing of one or more human drugs.Important facts regarding DMFs It is submitted to FDA to provide confidential informationIts submission is not required by law or regulationsIt is neither approved nor disapprovedIt is filed with FDA to support NDA, IND, ANDA another DMF or amendments and supplements to any of theseIt is provided for in the 21 CFR (Code of Federal Regulations) 314. 420It is not required when applicant references its own information.

9. What are the types of DMF's?

Ans-Type I: Manufacturing Site, Facilities, Operating Procedures, and Personnel (No longer accepted by FDA) Type II: Drug Substance, Drug Substance Intermediate, and Material Used in Their Preparation, or Drug Product Type III: Packaging Material Type IV: Excipient, Colorant, Flavour, Essence, or Material Used in Their Preparation Type V: FDA Accepted Reference Information (FDA discourages its use).

10. What is a 505 (b) (2) application?

Ans- 505 (b)(2) application is a type of NDA for which one or more investigations relied on by applicant for approval were not conducted by/for applicant and for which applicant has not obtained a right of reference.

11. What kind of application can be submitted as a 505(b) (2) application?

Ans- New chemical entity (NCE)/new molecular entity (NME) Changes to previously approved drugs

12.   What are the examples of changes to approved drug products for which 505(b) (2) application should be submitted?

Ans- Change in dosage form.

➢ Change in strength

➢ Change in route of administration Substitution of an active ingredient in a formulation product

➢ Change in formulation

➢ Change in dosing regimen

➢ Change in active ingredient new combination Product

➢ New indication

➢ Change from prescription indication to OTC indication

➢ Naturally derived or recombinant active ingredient

➢ Bioequivalence

13. What are the chemical classification codes for NDA?

➢ Number Meaning

New molecular entity (NME)

New ester, new salt, or other monovalent derivative

New formulation

New combination

New manufacturer

New indication

Drug already marketed, but without an approved NDA

➢ OTC (over-the-counter) switch

14. What are the differences between NDA and 505 (b) (2) application?

Ans- S.No.New Drug Application (NDA) 505 (b) (2) Application

➢ All investigations relied on by applicant for approval were conducted by/for applicant and for which applicant has right of reference One or more investigation relied on by applicant for approval were not conducted by/for applicant and for which applicant has not obtained a right of reference

➢ Generally, filed for newly invented pharmaceuticals. Generally, filed for new dosage form, new route of administration, new indication etc for all already approved pharmaceutical. Note: 505 (b) (2) application is a type of NDA.

15. What is a Marketing Authorization Application?

Ans- It is an application filed with the relevant authority in the Europe (typically, the UK's MHRA or the EMA's Committee for Medicinal Products for Human Use (CHMP)) to market a drug or medicine. As per UK's MHRA- Applications for new active substances are described as 'full applications'. Applications for medicines containing existing active substances are described as 'abbreviated' or 'abridged applications'.

16. What is an ASMF?

Ans-Active substance master file is a submission which is made to EMA, MHRA or any other Drug Regulatory Authority in Europe to provide confidential intellectual property or 'know-how' of the manufacturer of the active substance. In simple words, "It is a submission made to European Drug regulatory agencies on the confidential information of Active Substance or Active pharmaceutical Ingredient (API)".

17. What are the types of active substances for which ASMFs are submitted?

Ans-New active substances existing active substances not included in the European Pharmacopoeia (Ph. Eur.) or the pharmacopoeia of an EU Member State Pharmacopeial active substances included in the Ph. Eur. or in the pharmacopoeia of an EU Member State.

18. What is the difference between DMF and ASMF (with respect to submission)?

Ans-ASMF is submitted as Applicant's Part (Open Part) and Restricted Part (Closed Part) there isn't any differentiation of DMF's into parts.

19. What is ICH?

Ans-International Conference on Harmonisation of Technical Requirements for Registration of Pharmaceuticals for Human Use (ICH): is a project that brings together the regulatory authorities of Europe, Japan and the United

States and experts from the pharmaceutical industry in the three regions to discuss scientific and technical aspects of pharmaceutical product registration.

20. What is CTD?

Ans-The Common Technical Document (CTD) is a set of specification for application dossier, for the registration of Medicines and designed to be used across Europe, Japan and the United States. Quality, Safety and Efficacy information is assembled in a common format through CTD .The CTD is maintained by the International Conference on Harmonisation of Technical Requirements for Registration of Pharmaceuticals for Human Use (ICH).CTD format for submission of drug registration applications/dossiers is widely accepted by regulatory authorities of other countries too like Canada, Australia etc.

21. What are the ICH guidelines to be referred for preparation of registration dossiers/applications of medicines (With respect to format and contents in each module)?

➢ M4 Guideline

➢ M4Q Guideline

➢ M4S Guideline

➢ M4E Guideline

22. What are the modules in CTD?

Ans- the Common Technical Document is divided into five modules:

- Module 1. Administrative information and prescribing information
- Module 2. Common Technical Document summaries (Overview and summary of modules 3 to 5)
- Module 3. Quality
- Module 4. Nonclinical Study Reports (toxicology studies)
- Module 5. Clinical Study Reports (clinical studies)

22. What is Orange Book?

Ans-It is the commonly used name for the book "Approved Drug Products Equivalence Evaluations", which is published by USFDA.It contains the list of drug products, approved on the basis of safety and effectiveness by the Food and Drug Administration (FDA) under the Federal Food, Drug, and Cosmetic Act.

23. What is Hatch-Waxman act?

Ans-It is the popular name for Drug Price Competition and Patent Term Restoration Act, 1984. It is considered as the landmark legislation which established the modern system of generic drugs in USA. Hatch-Waxman amendment of the federal food, drug and cosmetics act established the process by which, would be marketers of generic drugs can file Abbreviated New Drug Application (ANDA) to seek FDA approval of generic drugs. Paragraph IV of the act, allows 180 day exclusivity to companies that are the "first-to-file" an ANDA against holders of patents for branded counterparts.In simple words "Hatch-Waxman act is the amendment to Federal, Food, Drug and Cosmetics act which established the modern system of approval of generics ".

24. What are the patent certifications under Hatch-Waxman act?

Ans-As per the Hatch and Waxman act, generic drug and 505 (b) (2) applicants should include certifications in their applications for each patent listed in the "Orange Book" for the innovator drug. This certification must state one of the following:(I) that the required patent information relating to such patent has not been filed (Para I certification);(II) that such patent has expired (Para II certification);(III) that the patent will expire on a particular date (Para III certification); or(IV) that such patent is invalid or will not be infringed by the drug, for which approval is being sought(Para IV certification).A certification under paragraph I or II permits the ANDA to be approved immediately, if it is otherwise eligible. A certification under paragraph III indicates that the ANDA may be approved when the patent expires.

25. What is meant by 180 day exclusivity?

Ans-The Hatch-Waxman Amendments provide an incentive of 180 days of market exclusivity to the "first" generic applicant who challenges a listed patent by filing a paragraph IV certification and thereby runs the risk of having to defend a patent infringement suit.180 Day Exclusivity could be granted to more than one applicant. The recent example is- 180 day exclusivity was granted to Ranbaxy and Watson Laboratories for marketing generic version of Lipitor (Atorvastatin calcium).

26. What are the procedures for Approval of Drug in EU?

➤ Centralised Procedure (CP)

➤ Decentralised Procedure (DCP)

➤ Mutual Recognition Procedure (MRP)

➤ National Procedure (NP)

27. What is the Full form of abbreviation, CEP?

Certificate of Suitability to the monographs of the European Pharmacopoeia (or) Certificate of suitability of monographs of the European Pharmacopoeia (or) Certification of suitability of European Pharmacopoeia monographs

It is also informally referred to as Certificate of Suitability (COS)

28. What is a CEP?

Ans. It is the certificate which is issued by Certification of Substances Division of European Directorate for the Quality of Medicines (EDQM), when the manufacturer of a substance provides proof that the quality of the substance is suitably controlled by the relevant monographs of the European Pharmacopoeia.

29. What are the recently approved new Drugs by FDA (Under NDA Chemical Type 1)? AS. NO. NDA NAME OF DRU GNAME OF ACTIVE INGREDIENT COMPANY

1203188	KALYDECOIVACAFT OR VERTEX PHARMS
2203388	ERIVEDGE VISMODEGIBGENEN TECH
3202324	INLYTA AXITINIBPFIZER
4202833	PICATOINGENOL MEBUTATELEO PHARMA AS
5202514	ZIOPTAN TAFLUPROSTMERCK SHARP DOHME
6021746	SURFAXINLUCINACTANT DISCOVERY LABORATORIES INC30.

NDA	New Drug Application
ANDA	Abbreviated New Drug application
IND	Investigational New Drug Application
DMF	Drug Master File
ASMF	Active Substance Master File
MAA	Marketing Authorisation Application
CEP	Certificate of Suitability to the monographs of the European Pharmacopoeia
ICH	The International Conference on Harmonisation of technical requirements for registration of Pharmaceuticals for human use.
CTD	Common technical document for the registration of pharmaceuticals for human use.
AP	Applicant's Part
RP	Restricted Part
OP	Open Part
CP	Closed Part
NME	New Molecular Entity
NCE	New Chemical Entity
SmPC	Summary of Product Characteristics
PL	Packaging Leaflet
RMS	Reference Member State
CMS	Concerned Member State
CHMP	The Committee for Medicinal Products for Human Use
CPMP	Committee for Proprietary Medicinal Products
CVMP	Committee for Medicinal Products for Veterinary Use
SUPAC	Scale-up and post approval changes

BACPAC	Bulk Active Chemicals Post approval Changes
cGMP	Current good Manufacturing Practice
GCP	Good clinical Practice
GLP	Good Laboratory Practice

31. Well known Drug Regulatory Agencies across the world-

NAME OF COUNTRY	REGULATORY AGENCIES
United States of America	United States Food and Drug Administration (USFDA)
United Kingdom	Medicines and Healthcare products Regulatory Agency (MHRA)
European Union	European Medicines Agency (EMA)
European Union	European Directorate for the Quality of Medicines (EDQM)
Australia	Therapeutic Goods Administration (TGA)
Canada	Therapeutic Products Directorate (TPD) in Health Product and food branch (HPFB) of Health Canada (HC)
Japan	Pharmaceutical and Medical Devices Agency (PMDA)
France	Agence Francaise de Securite Sanitaire des Produits de Sante (AFSSAPS)Translated into English as- French Agency for the Safety of Health Products
Germany	Bundesinstitut für Arzneimittel und Medizinprodukte, (BfArM) Tanslated into English as- Federal Institute for Drugs and Medical Devices
Brazil	Agência Nacional de Vigilância Sanitária (ANVISA) Tanslated into English as- The National Health Surveillance Agency

India	Drugs Controller General of India (DCGI) who heads Central Drugs Standard Control Organisation (CDSCO)
Switzerland	Swiss Agency for Therapeutic Products (SWISSMEDIC)
Singapore	Health Sciences Authority (HSA)

D & C ACT (1940) LIST OF AMENDING ACTS AND ADAPTATION ORDER

1. The Repealing and Amending Act, 1949 (40 of 1949).

2. The Adaptation of Laws Order, 1950.

3. The Part B States (Laws) Act, 1951 (3 of 1951)

4. The Drugs (Amendment) Act, 1955 (11 of 1955)

5. The Drugs (Amendment) Act, 1960 (35 of 1960)

6. The Drugs (Amendment) Act, 1962 (21 of 1962)

7. The Drugs and Cosmetics (Amendment) Act, 1964 (13 of 1964)

8. The Drugs and Cosmetics (Amendment) Act, 1972 (19 of 1972).

9. The Drugs and Cosmetics (Amendment) Act, 1982 (68 of 1982)

10. The Drugs and Cosmetics (Amendment) Act, 1986 (71 of 1986)

11. The Drugs and Cosmetics (Amendment) Act, 1995 (22 of 1995)

THE DRUGS AND COSMETICS ACT, 1940

ARRANGEMENT OF SECTIONS CHAPTER I

INTRODUCTORY

SECTIONS

1. Short title, extent and commencement.

2. Application of other laws not barred.

3. Definitions

   3A. Construction of references to any law not in force or any functionary not in existence in the State of Jammu and Kashmir.

4. Presumption as to poisonous substances.

CHAPTER II

THE DRUGS TECHNICAL ADVISORY BOARD, THE CENTRAL DRUGS LABORTORY AND THE DRUGS CONSULTATIVE COMMITTEE

5. The Drugs Technical Advisory Board.

6. The Central Drugs Laboratory.

7. The Drugs Consultative Committee.

7A. Section 5 and 7 not to apply Ayurvedic, Siddha or Unani drugs.

CHAPTER III

IMPORT OF DRUGS AND COSMETICS

8. Standards of quality

9. Misbranded drugs 9A. Adulterated drugs 9B. Spurious drugs.

9C. Misbranded cosmetics. 9D. Spurious cosmetics

10 Prohibition of import of certain drugs or cosmetics.

10A. Power of Central Government to prohibit import of drugs and cosmetics in public interest.

11. Application of law relating to sea customs and powers of Customs officers.

12 Power of Central Government to make rules.

13 Offences.

14 Confiscation

15. Jurisdiction

CHAPTER IV

MANUFACTURE, SALE AND DISTRIBUTION OF DRUGS AND COSMETICS SECTIONS

16. Standards of quality.

17. Misbranded drugs. 17A. Adulterated drugs. 17B. Spurious drugs.

17C. Misbranded cosmetics. 17D. Spurious cosmetics.

18. Prohibition of manufacture and sale of certain drugs and cosmetics. 18A. Disclosure of the name of the manufacturer, etc.

18B. Maintenance of records and furnishing of information.

19.   Pleas.

20.   Government Analysts.

21.   Inspectors.

22.   Powers of Inspectors.

23.   Procedure of Inspectors.

24.   Persons bound to disclose place where drugs or cosmetics are manufactured or kept.

25.   Reports of Government Analysts.

26.   Purchaser of drug or cosmetic enabled to obtain test or analysis.

26A.   Power of Central Government to prohibit manufacture etc. of drug and cosmetic in public interest.

27.   Penalty for manufacture, sale, etc., of drugs in contravention of this Chapter.

27A.   Penalty for manufacture, sale, etc., of cosmetics in contravention of this Chapter.

28.   Penalty for non-disclosure of the name of the manufacturer, etc.

28A.   Penalty for not keeping documents, etc., and for non-disclosure of information.

28B   Penalty for manufacture, etc. of drugs or cosmetics in contravention of section 26A.

29.   Penalty for use of Government Analyst's report for advertising.

30.   Penalty for subsequent offences.

31.   Confiscation.

31A.   Application of provisions to Government departments.

32.   Cognizance of offences.

32A.   Power of Court to implead the manufacturer, etc.

33.   Power of Central Government to make rules .

33A.   Chapter not to apply to Ayurvedic, Siddha or Unani drugs.

CHAPTER IVA

PROVISIONS RELATING TO AYURVEDIC SIDDHA AND UNANI DRUGS SECTIONS

33B. Application of Chapter IVA.

33C. Ayurvedic, Siddha and Unani Drugs Technical Advisory Board. 33D. The Ayurvedic, Siddha and Unani Drugs Consultative Committee. 33E. Misbranded drugs.

33EE. Adulterated drugs. 33EEA. Spurious drugs.

33EEB. Regulation of manufacture for sale of Ayurvedic, Siddha and Unani drugs.

33EEC. Prohibition of manufacture and sale of certain Ayurvedic, Siddha and Unani drugs. 33EED. Power of Central Government to prohibit manufacture etc., of Ayurvedic, Siddha or Unani drugs in public interest. 33F. Government Analysts.

33G. Inspectors .

33H. Application of provisions of sections 22, 23, 24 and 25.

33I. Penalty for manufacture, sale, etc., of Ayurvedic, Siddha or Unani drugs in contravention of this Chapter.

33J. Penalty for subsequent offences. 33K. Confiscation.

33L. Application of provisions to Government departments. 33M. Cognizance of offences.

33N. Power of Central Government to make rules. 33O. Power to amend First Schedule.

CHAPTER V MISCELLANEOUS

33P. Power to give directions.

34. Offences by companies.

34A. Offences by Government departments. 34AA. Penalty vexatious search or seizure.

35. Publication of sentences passed under this Act.

36. Magistrate's power to impose enhanced penalties.

36A.   Certain offences to be tried summarily.

37.   Protection of action taken in good faith.

38.   Rules to be laid before Parliament.

YEAR AND ACT

1970	Indian Patents Act
1919	Poison Act
1948	Pharmacy Act
1940	Drug and Cosmetic Act
1930	Dangerous Drug Act
1857	Opium Act
1954	Drug and Magic Remedies Act
1971	Medical Termination of Pregnancy Act (MTP)
1989	First ICH Indian pharmacopoeias:
1955	1st Edition IP
1966	2nd Edition IP

1985	3rd Edition IP
1996	4th Edition IP
2007	5th Edition IP
2010	6th Edition IP
2014	7th Edition IP

TECHNIQUE FOR NANOPARTICLE PREPARATION:

☐ Desolvation, denaturation

☐ Emulsion & interfecial polymerization

☐ Emulsification diiffusion

☐ Salting out.

STRENGTHS

☐ HCl (IP)-36

☐ H_2SO_4-12 N

IMP CHARACTERS:

- ☐ Nutmeg-Aril
- ☐ Stropanthus- Arista (Awn)
- ☐ Cardamon- Arilode
- ☐ Colchicum- Strophiole
- ☐ Castor- Caruncle

WHITEFIELD OINTMENT

- ☐ 6%benzoic acid
- ☐ 3%salicylic acid.
- ☐ Used as keratolytic.

SMART POLYMER:

- ☐ Polylactic acid
- ☐ Polyglycolic acid
- ☐ Poly-lactide co-glycolide
- ☐ Poly (dl-lactide-co-caprolactone)
- ☐ N-isopropylacrylamide

Difference between Aldol condensation & Cannizaro reaction:

- ☐ If aldehyde & ketone have alpha proton than Aldol condensation occur.
- ☐ If not, than cannizaro reaction occurs.

➢ **SOME IMPORTANT NOTES FOR GPAT EXAM**

➢ Betonite - derivative of monmorillonite.

➢ Hydrocaprolic acid-cyclic unsat fatty acid.

➢ Glucose-No UV abs.

➢ Vitamin B6 deficiency- sideroblastic anemia

➢ Smell of acetophenone when lobelia leaves burn.

➢ Rauwolfia tetraphylla devoid of recinnamine.

➢ Bromhexin- semisynthetic from vasaka.

➢ All electron withdrawing functional group are generally Meta directing except halogen group

➢ Stability order of carbocation is 3>2>1…

- Herceptin is Antineoplastic agent which cause CHF.
- Rasagaline is free from amphetamine prop due 2 aminoindane metabolite
- Rheumatoid factor is usually Ig M.
- Ca. sandoz is product of NOVARTIS.
- Phosphate is salt of Codeine.
- Seed of Indrajav is kurchi
- Transferosome are liposome used to increase Transdermal Permeation, in this deformability achieved by using surfactant in proper ratio.
- Abacavir, a nucleoside reverse transcriptse inhibitor NRTI is converted to which active metabolite?? Ans is Carbovir triphosphate.
- Cholesterol used in liposomes because it fills gaps created by imperfect packing of lipids when protein are embeded in membrane.
- Clenbutrol - anabolic drug uesd illicitly by athletes 2 improve performance
- For chest infection in asthma-clarithromycin used.
- Lotaustralin- isoleucin
- Squill, Manna, Psyllium Contain Trisaccharide.
- Diluents can be used in ratio 5-10% in tablet.
- In MRI max of 1.5 tesla magnetic field strength can be used.
- Lutrol is known as intelligent polymer.
- Chemical shift-independent of magnetic field
- Secondary structure of protein-alfa-beta helix
- 1960-prevention of cruelty to animals act.
- 1963-CPCSEA came into existence.
- 1998-breeding of and experimentation on animals act.
- Hydrolysis of ethyl acetate is pseudo first order reaction
- Suspensions follow pseudo zero order reaction
- Cis form gives 5-12 delta value and trans form gives 12-18 delta value in NMR
- Polystyrene and water are both used as standard for calibration of IR
- B-cyclodextrin has max Solubility
- H-bond can detected by IR & NMR

- Free radicals are identified by E.S.R (electron spin resonance)
- TRIPS-trade related aspects of intellectual property rights
- TRIMS-trade related investment measures
- WIPO-world intellectual property organisation.
- Seliwanoffs reagent contain resorcinol + glacial acetic acid.
- Lucas reagent HCl+ZnCl2.
- Ames test to detect carcinogenicity
- Nitrocellulose is used as base in nail lacquers.
- Nucleosome contain DNA with histone protein in ratio 30:1
- Neumanns test is used for the identification of Casein.
- Gaultheria con. Methyl salicylate.
- PULSED FLOW IS THE disadvantage of reciprocating pump in HPLC.
- *P.bracteatum* do not contain morphine.
- **BENTING & BEST** founded insulin.
- H1N1-'N' stands for Neuramidase.
- Fiehls test is used for determination of sucrose
- Shinoda test for identification of flavanoids.
- Murexide test for caffeine.
- Bacteria need 0.5%NaCl for maintaining isotonicity not 0.9% NaCl.
- RITONAVIR IS also known as pharmacokinetic enhancer. Because it increases bioavailability of antiviral drugs.
- Banana bond is the characteristic of cyclopropane.
- Caffine is Pseudo tannin.
- Rivastigmine is used in Alzheimer's disease and it is a pseudo irreversible inhibitor of cholinesterase enzyme.
- Carvedilol-a mixed adrenoceptor antagonist has antioxidant effect also.
- Minoxidil-K channel opener + release NO.
- Liquid Nitrogen temperature is -197 degree Celcius.
- Caco2, a cell line model is used to classify drug for its BCS
- Classification bleomycin & nitrosourea coming under cycle nonspecific anticancer Agent

- All xanthophylline act on Adenosine receptor except enrophylline.
- Omalizumab used in asthma, it is anti IgE antibody.

BIOCHEMISTRY IMPORTANT PINPOINTS

- A living cell is true representative of life with its own organization & specialized Functions.
    - Accumulation of lipofuscin, a pigment rich in lipids and proteins, in the cell has been Implicated in ageing process.
- Leakage of lysosomal enzymes into the cell degrades several functional macromolecules and this may lead to certain disorders (e.g. arthritis).
- Zellweger syndrome is rare disease characterized by the absence of functional peroxisome.
- Lysosomes are the digestive bodies of the cell, actively involved in the degradation of Cellular compounds. Peroxisomes contain the enzyme cataloes that protects the cell from the toxic effects of H_2O_2.
- The cellular ground matrix is referred to as cytosol which, in fact, is composed of a network of protein filaments, the cytoskeleton.
- **Mutarotation:** The Anomers of glucose have different optical rotations. The specific optical rotation of a freshly prepared glucose (anomer) solution in water is $+112.2^O$ which gradually changes and attains an equilibrium with a constant value of $+52.7^O$. In the presence of alkali, the decrease in optical rotation is rapid. The optical rotation of p-glucose is **+18.7° (19°)**
- **Mutarotation of fructose:** Fructose also exhibits Mutarotation. Ln case of fructose, the pyranose ring (six-membered) is converted to furanose (five-membered) ring, till an equilibrium is attained. And fructose has a specific optical rotation of **-92°** at equilibrium
- **von Gierke's disease (type ii):** The incidence of type I glycogen storage disease is 1 per 200,000 persons. It is transmitted by autosomal recessive trait. This disorder results in various biochemical manifestation
- **Anderson's disease (amylopectinosis):** A rare disease, glycogen with only few branches accumulate; cinhosis of liver, impairment in liver function.

- ➤ **Pompe's disease:** Glycogen accumulates in lysosomes in almost all the tissues; heart is mostly involved; enlarged liver and heart, nervous system is also affected; death occurs at an early age due to heart failure.
- ➤ **Cori's disease:** Branched chain glycogen accumulates; liver enlarged; clinical manifestations are similar but milder compared to von Gierke's disease.

Distinct deficiency conditions of certain b-complex vitamins are known

VITAMIN	DEFICIENCY
Thiamine	Beriberi
Niacin	Pellagra
Riboflavin	Cheilosis, glossitis
Pyridoxine	Peripheral neuropathy
Folic acid	Macrocytic anemia
Cobalomin	Pernicious anemia

- ➤ B-complex vitamin deficiencies are usually multiple rather than individual with overlapping symptoms.
- ➤ A combined therapy of vitamin B12 and folic acid is commonly employed to treat the patients of megaloblostic anaemias.
- ➤ Megodoses of niacin are useful in the treatment of hyperlipidemia.
- ➤ Long term use of isoniazid for the treatment of tuberculosis causes 86 deficiency.
- ➤ Folic acid supplementation reduces elevated plasma homocysteine level which is Associated with atherosclerosis and thrombosis.
- ➤ Sulfonamides serve as antibacterial drugs by inhibiting the incorporation of PABA to produce folic acid.
- ➤ Aminopterin and amethopterin, the structural analogues of folic acid, are employed in the treatment of cancers.

➤ Lipoic acid is therapeutically useful as an antioxidant to present stroke, myocardial infarction, etc.

<u>Colour reactions of proteins/amino acids Reaction Specific group or amino acid</u>

REACTION	SPECIFIC GROUP OR AMINO ACID
Biuret reaction	Two peptide linkages
Ninhydrin reaction	☐-Amino acids
Xanthoproteic Reaction	Benzene ring of aromatic amino acids (Phe, Tyr, Trp)
Millons reaction	Phenolic group(Tyr)
Hopkins-Cole Reaction	Indole ring (Trp)
Sakaguchi reaction	Guanidino group (Arg)
Nitroprusside reaction	Sulfhydryl groups (Cys)
Sulfur test	Sulfhydryl groups (Cys)
Pauly's test	Imidazole ring (His)
Folin coicalteau's test	Phenolic groups (Tyr)

DRUGS OF CHOICE

1. Paracetamol poisoning- acetyl cysteine
2. Acute bronchial asthma: - salbutamol
3. Acute gout: - NSAIDS
4. Acute hyperkalemia: - calcium gluconate
5. Severe DIGITALIS toxicity: - DIGIBIND
6. Acute migraine: - sumatriptan
7. Cheese reaction: - phentolamine
8. Atropine poisoning: - physostigmine
9. Cyanide poisoning: - amyl nitrite
10. Benzodiazepine poisoning: - flumazenil
11. Cholera: - tetracycline

12. KALA-AZAR:- lipozomal amphotericin- B

13. Iron poisoning: - desferrioxamine -

14. MRSA: - vancomycin

15. VRSA: - LINEZOLID

16. Warfarin overdose: - vitamin-K (NIPER- 2009)

17. OCD: - fluoxetine

18. Alcohol poisoning: - fomepizole

19. Epilepsy in pregnency: - Phenobarbitone

20. Anaphylactic shock: - Adrenaline

21. MRSA Infection-Vancomycin

22. Malaria in Pregnancy-Chloroquine

23. Whooping Cough or Pertussis- Erythromycin

24. Kawasaki disease-IV Ig

25. Warfarin Overdose-Vit-K

26. Heparin Overdose-Protamine

27. Hairy Cell Leukemia-Cladirabine

28. Multiple Myeloma- Melphalan

29. CML-Imatinib

30. Wegner's granulomatosis-Cyclophosphamide

31. HOCM- Propranolol

32. Delirium Tremens-Diazepam

33. Drug Induced Parkinsonism-Benzhexol

34. Diacumarol Poisoning-Vit-K

35. Type-1 Lepra Reaction-Steroids

36. Type- 2 Lepra Reaction-Thalidomide

37. Allergic Contect Dermatitis-Steroids

38. PSVT- 1st-Adenosine, 2nd-Verapamil, 3rd-Digoxin

39. Z-E Syndrome- Proton Pump Inhibitor

40. Chancroid-Cotrimoxazole

41. Dermatitis Herpetiformis-Dapsone

42. Spastic Type of Cerebral Palsy-Diazepam

43. Herpis Simplex Keratitis-Trifluridine

44. Herpes Simplex Orolabialis-Pancyclovir

45. Neonatal Herpes Simplex-Acyclovir

46. Pneumocystis carinii Pneumonia- Cotrimoxazole for Nodulo

47. Cystic Acne- Retinoic acid

48. Trigeminal Neuralgia-Carbamezapine

49. Actinomycosis-Penicillin

50. Plague- Streptomycin

51. Opioid Withdrawal- Methadone 2nd-Clonidine

52. Alcohol Withdrawal- Chlordiazepoxide 2nd-Diazepam

53. Post Herpetic Neuralgia- Fluphenazine

54. WEST Syndrome-ACTH

55. Diabetic Diarrhoea- Clonidine

56. Lithium Induced Neuropathy-Amiloride Communicable Disease:

57. Tetanus: PEN G Na; TETRACYCLINE; (DIAZEPAM

58. Diphteria: PEN G K; ERYTHROMYCIN

59. Pertusis: ERYTHROMYCIN; AMPICILLIN

60. Meningitis: MANNITOL (osmotic diuretic); DEXAMETHASONE (anti-inflammatory); DILANTIN/PHENYTOIN (anti-convulsive); PYRETINOL/ENCEPHABOL (CNS stimulant)

61. Cholera: TETRACYCLINE

62. Amoebic Dysentery: METRONIDAZOLE

63. Shigellosis: CO-TRIMOXAZOLE

64. Typhoid: CHORAMPHENICOL

65. Rabies: LYSSAVAC, VERORAB

66. Immunoglobulins: ERIG or HRIg

67. Malaria: CHLOROQUINE

68. Schistosomiasis: PRAZIQUANTEL

69. Felariasis: DIETHYLCARBAMAZINE CITRATE

70. Scabies: EURAX/ CROTAMITON

71. Chicken pox: ACYCLOVIR/ZOVIRAX

72.   Leptospirosis: PENICILLIN; TETRACYCLINE; ERYTHROMYCIN

73. Leprosy: DAPSONE, RIFAMPICIN

74. Anthrax: PENICILLIN

75. Tuberculosis: R.I.P.E.S.

76. Pneumonia: COTRIMOXAZOLE; Procaine, Penicillin

77. Helminths: MEBENDAZOLE; PYRANTEL, PAMOATE

78.   Meningitis: MANNITOL (dec. ICP); DEXAMETHASONE (relieve cerebral edema); DIAZEPAM (anticonvulsant); PENICILLIN

79. Syphilis: PENICILLIN

80. Gonorrhoea: PENICILLIN

<u>Classification of antimicrobial agents: On the basis of their mechanism of action</u> Antimicrobial agents are used for the treatment of the microbial infections in the body and the treatment is termed as chemotherapy. Paul Ehlrich is known as the father of Chemotherapy who used Arsphenamine for the treatment of Syphilis. Chemotherapy is an important perspective for the student's GPAT preparation as lots of questions are asked from this section. Here, we are introducing the classification of antimicrobial agents on the basis of their mechanism of action.

Classification of antimicrobial agents

1. <u>Antibiotics that inhibits Bacterial Cell Wall synthesis</u>

- **Pencillins,**
- **Cephalosporins**
- **Carbepenam**

  - **Monobactam Mechanism:**

<u>These drugs inhibit the transpeptidase enzyme used in the bacterial cell wall synthesis.</u>

  - **Vancomycin Mechanism:**

<u>This drug makes complex with C-terminal D-alanine residues of peptidoglycan precursors.</u>

  - **Cycloserine Mechanism:**

<u>It inhibits alanine racemase and D-alanyl-D-alanine synthetase.</u>

2. **Antibiotics that inhibit Ribosome function and prevent protein synthesis**

a) Aminoglycosides: It causes misreading in mRNA

b)   Tetracyclines: This class of drug binds with 30S ribosomes and inhibits the binding of aminoacyl-tRNA into the A site of the bacterial ribosome.

c)   Chloramphenicol: It binds with the peptidyl transferase enzyme on the 50S ribosome and inhibits protein synthesis.

d) Spectinomycin

e)   Azithromycin and Clarithromycin: Inhibits translocation which leads the protein synthesis inhibition.

3.   Antibiotics that affect the function of cytoplasmic membranes a) Antifungal drugs:

- ☐ Amphotericin B
- ☐ Ketoconazole
- ☐ Clotrimazole
- ☐ Fluconazole
- ☐ Miconazole
- ☐ Nystatin.

b) Bacitracin & Polymyxin B & E:

They cause the leaking of nuclear material which leads to the cell death.

c) Gramicidin: It produces aqueous pores in the cell membrane.

4. **Antibiotics that inhibit Nucleic acid synthesis**

a) Agents that interfere with Nucleotide synthesis:

- Zidovudine: DNA polymerase inhibition.
- Acyclovir: Thymidine kinase and DNA polymerase inhibition of Herpes virus.
- Flucytosine: Thymidylate synthetase inhibition.

b) Agents that interfere with DNA replication:

- Metronidazole: DNA strand breakage by the reduced Nitro group.
- Quinolones: DNA gyrase inhibition

c) Agents that inhibit RNA polymerase:

- Rifamycin

d) <u>Agents that interfere with the precursor synthesis:</u>

Sulfonamides: Inhibit the conversion of Pteridine & p-Amino Benzoic acid (PABA) into dihydrofolic acid.

Trimethoprim: Inhibits the conversion dihydrofolic acid into tetrahydrofolic acid.

e) <u>Agents that interfere with the Template function of DNA:</u>

<u>PHARMACOLOGY</u>

<u>Pharmacodynamics</u>	: - What drug does to body.
<u>Pharmacokinetics</u>	: - What body does to the drug.
<u>Pharmacotherapeutics</u>	: - Use of drugs in treatment of disease.
<u>Clinical pharmacology</u>	: - Scientific study of drugs in man.
<u>Toxicology</u>	: - Aspect of pharmacology deals with

adverse effects of Drugs.

<u>Pharmacodynamic agents</u> : - Designed to have pharmacodynamic effects in the recipient.

<u>Chemotherapeutic agents</u> : - Designed to inhibit/kill parasites/malignant cells & does not have or with minimal pharmacodynamic effects in recipient.

<u>Orphan drugs</u> : - Drugs or Biological Products for diagnosis/treatment/ Prevention of a rare disease.

E.g.:- Liothyronine (T3), Desmopressin, Baclofen, Digoxin Antibody.

<u>Routes of drug Administration</u>

1) Oral 2) Parentral

<u>Injections:-</u>

A) <u>Intradermal</u>: - given in to layers of skin. E.g.:- BCG vaccine, for testing drug sensitivity.

B) <u>S.C:-</u> Only non-irritant drug are given absorption can be enhanced by enzyme Hyalurinase S.C.drug implants can act as depot therapy. E.g.:- steroid hormones.

In children saline is injected in large quantities – Hypodermalysis.

C) <u>I.M:-</u> Mild irritants, suspensions & colloids can be injected by this route.

D) <u>I.V:-</u> Directly to vein.

E) <u>Intra arterial: -</u> Only used for diagnostic studies. E.g.:- Angiograms, embolism therapy.

F) <u>Intrathecal: -</u> Spinal anaesthetics in to subarachinoid space.

G) <u>Intra medullary: -</u> Drug introduced to Bone marrow.

H) <u>Intra articular & Intra tensional: -</u> Drug administered into joints. E.g.:- Hydrocortisone acetate in rheumatoid arthritis.

PHARMACOKINETICS

Absorption of Drugs:-

A) **Simple diffusion:** - Bidirectional process rate of transfer across the membrane is proportional to concn gradient. E.g.:- H_2O soluble drugs with low mol-wt, lipid soluble drugs.

B) **Active transport:** - requires energy – independent of physical properties of membrane. E.g.:- H_2O soluble drugs with high mol-wt.

Carrier mediated transport: - E.g.:- Intestinal absorption of Ca^{2+}.

C) **Pinocytosis:** - Important in unicellular organisms like Amoeba.

Bioavailability: - Amount of drug reaches systemic circulation following a non-vascular drug administration.

<u>AUC Oral</u> F = AUC IV

Barriers:-

:- made up of choroid cells (strong Barrier). <u>Testis Barrier:</u> - made up of seroid cells.

<u>Placental Barrier:</u> - made up of sertoli cells (weak Barrier). <u>Endothelial Barrier:</u> - in all blood cells (very weak).

For absorption of $vitB_{12}$, **IF** factor is required which is synthesized by parietal cells?

Solubility of drugs:-

Ionized form – soluble Unionized form – more absorbed

Distribution of drugs:-

<u>Plasma protein binding:</u> - many drugs have affinity towards plasma proteins,

Acidic drugs towards Albumin, Basic drugs towards acid Glycoprotein, Prothrombin, and Thromboplastin.

Radioligand binding: - is used to determine drug in protein complex.

PPB V_d

Tissue storage of drugs:-

Skeletal muscle, Heart: - Digoxin, emetine Liver: - Chloroquine, tetracycline's, digoxin Kidney: - Chloroquine, digoxin, emetine Thyroid: - Iodine

Brain: - CPZ, Acetazolamide, Isoniazid Retina: - Chloroquine

Iris: - Ephedrine, Atropine

Bone & Teeth: - Heavymetals, Tetracycline's

Adipose tissue: - Phenoxy Benzamine, Minocycline, ether, Thiopentane.

Metabolism of drugs :- (Biotransformation / Detoxification)

Chemical alteration of drug in physiological system

1. Inactive form

2. Active metabolite, E.g.:- Codeine to morphine

3. Prodrug to active drug, E.g.:- L-Dopa to Dopamine

Phase I metabolism: - Nonsynthetic

Reaction	Enzyme	Examples
Oxdn	Monooxygenases cytp450 in lives	Drugs with "OH" & "COOH" groups
Redn	Reductases	Halothane, trichloroethand
Hydrolysis	Esterases	Lidocaine procainide Benzocaine
Cyclisation		Proguanil to cycloguanil
Decyclisation		Phenobarbitone & Phenytoin

Phase II Metabolism: - Synthetic or Conjugation

Conjugation	Endogenous substrate	Examples
1. Glucouronide	Glucouronic acid (glucose)	"Oh" & "COOH" group drugs
2. Acetylation	Acetyl co-A (Citric acid cycle)	"NH_2" & Hydrazine group drugs
3. Methylation	Methionine	"NH_2" & Phenol group drugs

4. Sulphate	Sulfokinases	Phenolic compds & Steroids
5.Glycine(rarely occur)	Glycine	Salicylates & "COOH" group drugs
6. Glutathione		Paracetamol
7. Ribonucleotide		Purine & Pyrimidine antimetabolites

Prodrug	Active form	Active drug	Active Metabolite
Levodopa	Dopamine	Chloralhydrate	Trichloroethanol
Enalpril	Enalaprilat	Phenacetin	Paracetamol
L-Methyldopa	L-Methylnorepinephrine	Primidone	Phenobarbitone
Dipivefrine	Epinephrine	Digitoxin	Digoxin
Benorylate	Aspirin+Paracetamal	Codeine	Morphine
Proguanil	Proguanil triazine	Spironolactone	Canrenone
Prednisone	Prednisolone	Amitryptiline	Nor-tryptiline
Becampicillion	Ampicillin	Diazepam	Desmethyl;diazepam, oxazepam
Sulphasalazine	5-amino salicylic acid	Trimethadione	Dimethadione

Microsomal enzymes: - These are inducible by drugs, diet E.g.:- cytP$_{450}$, Monooxygenases, Glucouronyl transferase etc.

Catalyses many oxdn, redn, Hydrolysis & glucouronide conjugations.

Non Microsomal enzymes: - E.g.:- Flavoprotein oxidases, esterases, amidases & conjugases. Catalyses some oxdn & redn, many hydrolytic reactions & all conjugations except glucouronidation.

Hofmann elimination: - Inactivation of drug in body fluids by spontaneous molecular rearrangement without enzymes. E.g.:- Atracurium.

Enzyme inducers: - Phenytoin, Barbiturates, Rifampicin, Carbamazepine.

Enzyme Inhibitors: - Cimetidine, erythromycin, chloramphenicol, ciprofloxacin, MAO inhibitors, sulfonamides, verapamil, INH, Disulfiram etc.

<u>**Excretion of drugs:**</u> - elimination of drug in inactive form,

Urine – H_2O soluble drugs, Feces – Unabsorbed drugs (complex drugs insoluble drugs), Swets – salts & heavy metals,

Saliva – Hm, Lead, SCN, Lithium, & Tetracycline's, Lungs – gaseous drugs, Alcohol paraldehyde etc., Lacrimal – drugs applied to eye.

<u>Rate of elimination</u> Clearance = plasma concn of drug

PHARMACODYNAMICS

Drug produces action by stimulation, depression, irritation, replacements cytotoxic action.

<u>Mechanism of drug action:-</u>

	Properties	Drugs
Physical	Mass of drug Adsorptive property Osmotic activity Radioactivity Radio opacity	Bulk laxatives, protectives charcoal, kaolin $mgso_4$, mannitol I^{131} & other isotope $Baso_4$, urografin
Chemical	Neutralizing germicidal chelating	Antacids $Knmo_4$, I_2 EDTA, Penicillamine

<u>**Through enzymes:**</u> - Drugs may also increase or decrease rate of enzymatically mediated reactions.

<u>**Stimulation:**</u> - e.g.:- Adrenaline stimulates Adenyl cyclase pyridoxine increases decarboxylase activity.

a) <u>Inhibition :-</u>

1) <u>Non specific inhibition: -</u> Many drugs act by denaturing proteins. E.g.:- Hm, Acid & Alkalies, Alcohol, Formaldehyde, Phenol etc.

2) <u>**Specific inhibition :-**</u>

i) <u>Competitive:</u> - Physostigmine & neostigmine with Ach for sulfonamides with PABA for folatesynthetase Allopurinol with Hypoxanthine for xanthine oxidase carbidopa & methyldopa with L – Dopa for dopa decorboxylase.

ii) <u>Non-competitive:-</u> Ach & Papaverine on smooth muscles Ach & Decamethionine on NmJ.

<u>**Through receptors:-**</u>

1) <u>Clark-Arheneous theory (occupation theory):-</u> The effect of drug is proportional to fraction of receptors occupied by drug & maximum effect results when all receptors are occupied.

2) <u>Raton's theory (Rate theory):-</u> The effect of drug is a function of receptor occupation & the rate of drug receptor combination. Here response depends on rate of Association between drug molecule & receptor.

   G proteins are Heterotrimeric proteins involved in receptor transduction it has 3 subunits.

   $PAx = -\log (A)_x,$

   $PA2 = -\log (A)_2,$

   $PD2 = -\log (a)_2,$

   Where (A) = molar concn of antagonist, where (a) = molar concn of against.

   <u>Eudismic ratio: -</u> ratio of the activities of active enantiomer (eutomer) and inactive enantiomer (distomer) in chiral pharmocodynamics.

<u>AUTONOMIC NERVOUS SYSTEM</u>

Sympathetic or Adrenergic system enables the individual to adjust to stress & prepares the body for '**Fight or Flight**' response.

Parasympathetic or Cholinergic mainly participate in tissue building reactions.

Both sympathetic & parasympathetic nervous system consists of myelinated preganglionic fibre which forms a synapse with the cell body of non-myelinated post ganglionic fibre.

Synapse: - It is the structure formed by the close opposition of a neuron either with another neuron or with effector cells.

The synapse b/w preganglionic & postganglionic fibres is termed as Ganglion The synapse b/w postganglionic &receptors is termed as Neuroeffector junction.

Neurohumoral transmission: - The transmission of an impulse across the synapse in central & peripheral nervous system occurs as a result of release of a neurohumoral transmitter substance in to the synaptic cleft.

Junctional transmission: - The arrival of an action potential at the axonal terminals initiates the series of events that put in to effect neurohumoral transmission of an excitatory/inhibitory impulse across the synapse / neuroeffector junction.

ADRENERGIC RECEPTORS:-

Receptor	Agonist	Antagonist	Tissue	Response	Molecular mechanism
a_1	Methoxamine	Quinazoline derivatives (Prazosin)	Blood vessel Smooth muscle Liver	Vasoconstriction Contraction Increased blood glucose level	Stimulation of phospholipase- C & formation of IP_3 /DAG
a_2	Clonidine	Yohimbine. Raulosine	Islet cells Platelets Vascular smooth muscles	Decreased insulin Aggregation Contraction	Inhibition of Adenylcyclase & neuronal ca^{2+} channels
b_1	Dobutamine	Atenolol, Acebutolol, Bisoprolol, Metoprolol	Heart Juxta glomerular cells	$+^{ve}$ Inotropic actions Increased rennin release	Activation of Adenylcyclase
b_2	Terbutaline, salbutamol	Butoxamine Methyl Propranalol	Smooth muscles	Relaxation	Activation of Adenylcyclase
b_3	Sibutramine (Antiobesity)	-------------	Adipose tissue	Lipolysis	Activation of Adenylcyclase

Adrenergic receptors are membrane bound G- Protein coupled receptors which function primarily by increasing/decreasing the intracellular production of secondary messengers' $cAMP/IP_3$- DAG. In some cases the activated G-Protein itself operates K^+/Ca^{2+} channels or increases prostaglandin production.

Classification of Adrenergic drugs:-

A. Therapeutic classification-

1. Pressor drugs: - Adrenaline, NA, Metarminol
2. Inotropic agents: - Dopamine, Dobutamine, Isoprenaline& Xamoterol

3. CNS Stimulants:-Amphetamine

4. Smooth muscle relaxants:-Adrenaline, Isoprenaline, Isoxsuprine& b_2 stimulants (Salbutamol)

5. Drugs used in allergy: - Adrenaline & ephedrine

6. Local vasoconstrictor effect:-Adrenaline, Naphozoline, Phenylephrine

7. Nasal decongestants: - Oxymetazoline, Tuaminoheptanesulfate

8. Anorectics: - Fenfluramine, dexfenfluramine&Phenteramine

9. Antiobesity: - Sibutramine

B. Chemical classification:-

1. Catecholamines – Adrenaline, NA, Dopamine, 5-HT & Isoprenaline

2. Non-Catecholamines – Amphetamine, Ephedrine, Isoxsuprine, Mephentamine

Pharmacological Actions:-

1. **Heart**: - Due to its stimulant action on b_1 receptors causes $+^{ve}$ inotropic actions. This is associated with increased metabolism of myocardium & increased O_2 consumption, thus decreasing cardiac efficiency.

2. **Blood vessels**: - Raises systolic B.P. by its cardiac actions lowers diastolic B.P. by its peripheral actions & hence not suitable in Hypotensive shock

➢ In moderate doses rise in B.P. is followed by a fall as it activates both the receptors. This is called as 'Biphasic response'.

➢ By prior administration of **a** blockers (ergot) leads to stimulation of only b_2 receptors & thus causes a fall in B.p. This phenomenon is called as 'Dale's vasomotor reversal'

Compared to Adrenaline, the NA has feeble actions on b_2 receptors.

3. **Smooth muscles**: - relaxes bronchial muscles

Produce contraction of spleemic capsule producing a release of erythrocytes in to the Peripheral circulation. This serves as protective mechanism during stress such as hypoxia & Hemorrhage

4. **Eye**: - Mydriasis due to contraction of radial muscle fibres of IRIS. On topical application do not produce Mydriasis but cause reduction in

intraocular tension.

5. **Respiration**: - Bronchodilator & weak stimulant

6. **Metabolic effects**: - Increases Blood glucose, Blood lactate, free fatty acids. Inhibits insulin release.

7. **CNS**: - Catecholamines cannot cross BBB

8. **Miscellaneous**: - Skeletal muscle contraction, Accelerates Blood coagulation, Platelet aggregation, Leucocytosis& Eosonopenia. Inhibit cellular anaphylactic mechanism& prevent release of allergic mediators (Histamine from mast cells)

Major excretory products are Vanillin mandelic acid

Therapeutic Uses:-

1. Na in elevating B.P. in shock

2. In glaucoma. To control hemorrhage

3. Cardiac resuscitation

4. Bronchial asthma

5. First line drug in Hypersensitivity

6. Along with Local anaesthetics to prolong their action.

Note: - Metyltyrosine/Metyrosine/2-methyl p-tyrosine inhibits Tyrosine hydroxylase in synthesis of catecholamines & used in treatment of Pheocytochroma.

Catecholamines	Non-catecholamines
Not effective orally Do not cross BBB Susceptible to MAO	Orally effective Crosses BBB Relatively resistant to MAO

Nasal decongestants: - Most of the Sympathetic amines on topical application produce Local vasoconstriction & used as Decongestants

E.g. Oxymetazoline, Zylometazoline, Naphozoline.tuaminoheptanesulfate

Potency of agonists at a&b receptors are-

a- Adrenaline > NA > Isoprenaline

b- Isoprenaline > Adrenaline > NA

b$_2$ selective receptor stimulants: -

- Isoprenaline used in Asthma will cause adverse cardiac effects due to action on b_1
- Therefore selective b_2 stimulants are used in Asthma & as Tocolytics
- E.g.Nylidrin.Isoxsuprine

Drugs used in CCF:-

- Dopamine& Dopexamine acts on **a & b** receptors as well as D_1&D_2 receptor.
- Dobutamine acts only on **a &b** receptor
- Xamoterol has selective b_1 agonist action.

ADRENERGIC BLOCKING AGENTS:-

Classification:-

-Blockers:-

1. - Haloalkylamines- Dibenamine& Phenoxybenzamine
2. Imidazoline derivatives- Tolazoline& Phentolamine
3. Quinazolines- Prazosin, terazosin, tremazosin
4. Natural & dehydrogenated ergot alkaloids
5. Miscellaneous- yohimbine, Indoramine, Cpz

   The receptor blockade produced by Dibenamine& Phenoxybenzamine is irreversible type. Phenoxybenzamine is 6-10 times more potent than Dibenamine but has be converted to active metabolite.

   Therapeutics Uses: - In pheocytochroma, Hypertension, Secondary shock, CHF, BHP, Male sexual dysfunction, Scorpion Bite.

-Blockers:-

1. Specific **b**- Blockers- Timolol, Nadolol
2. Blockers with membrane stabilizing action: - Propranalol, Oxyprenolol, Pindolol
3. Blockers with cardioselective action: - Atenolol, Acebutolol, Metoprolol&Esmolol
4. Both **a &b** blockers: - Labetolol, Carvedilol, Dilevilol&Medroxolol

   Atenolol with poor lipid solubility does not cross BBB at all.

   Propranolol, Alprenolol&Metoprolol are metabolized by liver, Practolol is largely excreted unchanged by kidneys.

- Pindolol, Atenolol, Acebutolol& Timolol by both the routes.
- They are contraindicated in the myocardial insufficiency, Bradycardia, Asthma, Heartblock& Insulin dependent diabetes.

T.Uses:-Anginapectoris, MI, Cardiac arrhythmia, Hypertension, Thyrotoxicosis, Pheocytochroma, to decrease cardiac symptoms prior to important speech/meetings.

Propranalol is useful in prevention of Migrane & treatment of Essential tumor.

CHOLINERGIC DRUGS

Ach produces its dual actions as Muscarinic actions on Muscarinic & Nicotinic actions on nicotinic receptors.

Muscarinic receptors (mol, wt-80,000) belong to g-Protein coupled receptors.

Nicotinic receptors are Pentameric proteins.

Receptors	Agonist	Antagonist	Tissue	Response	Molecular Mechanism
N_m	Phenyl trimethyl ammonia	D-Tc a-Bangarotoxin	NMJ	End depolarization	Opening of cation channels
N_n	Dimethyl phenyl piperazinum	Trimethophan Hexamethonium Succinylcholine	Autonomic Ganglia Adrenal medulla	Depolarization& firing of catecholamines	Opening of cation channels
M_1	Oxytremonium	Pirenzepine Telenzepine Atropine	Autonomic Ganglia Gastric Glands	Depolarisation	Stimulation of phospholipase- C & formation of IP_3 /DAG

| M_2 | Methacholine | Methocrotamine Atropine | Heart | Negative Inotropic effect | Inhibition of Adenylcyclase |
| M_3 | Bethnecol | Atropine Hexahydrosilede nifol | Smooth Muscles Secretory Glands | Contraction Increased secretion | Stimulation of phospholipase- C & formation of IP_3 /DAG |

CLASSIFICATION:-

1. Esters of Choline – Ach, Methacholine, Carbachol& Bethnechol

2. Cholinomimetic Alkaloids – Pilocarpine, Muscarine&Arecholine

3. Cholinesterase inhibitors –

a)   Reversible: - Physostigmine (Natural), Neostigmine.Pyridostigmine, demecarium Tacrine (Acridine) used in Alzhmeir's disease.

b)   Ir-reversible: - Di-isopropylflurophosphate (therapeutically useful), OMPP, Malathion, Parathion, Nerve gases (Tabun, sarin& Soman) Propoxur (carbamates)

Pharmacological actions:- Undergoes Hydrolysis in Neutral or Alkaline medium & hence preserved in Acidic medium.

On oral administration gets destroyed by GIT & hence given by I.v. There is no circulating Ach in the Blood.

Muscarinic actions –

1.   **CVS**: - Negative Inotropic actions, Dilates Blood vessels, Coronary arteries&veins. Increases tone & rhythmic activity of smooth muscles of GIT & enhance Peristalsis.

2.   **Secretions**: - Increases Nasal, Bronchial, Gastric, salivary, Pancreatic & Intestinal secretions.

3. **Eye**: - on instillation no effect. But on injection to carotid arteries produces- Constriction of Pupil (Miosis) – By contracting circular fibres of sphincter pupillae

Spasm of accommodation – Due to contraction of ciliary muscle, resulting in relaxation of suspensory ligament of lens.

Nicotinic actions –

1. Increases output of Ach&NA from Post ganglionic sympathetic & Parasympathetic nerve endings & increases B.p.

2. Produce paralysis of skeletal muscles at NMJ

Contraindications of choline esters: - Hyperthyroidism, Bronchial asthma, Peptic ulcer& MI

T.Uses: - Glaucoma, Post operative paralytic ileus & abdominal distension

Anticholinesterases: - they act by inhibiting true & Pseudo cholinesterases, thus causing accumulation of Ach at various sites.

MOA: - Ach is inactivated by combination of 2 sites on enzyme Cholinesterase.

Anionic site bearing $-^{ve}$ charge attracts Quaternary nitrogen atom of Ach

Esteratic site which attracts carboxylic acid group of Ach. As a result of union of Ach with cholinesterase the esteratic site of enzyme is acetylated & this results in splitting of choline. The acetyl group in combination with esteratic site is However immediately removed as a result of combination with water forming Acetic acid.

This sets esteratic site of enzyme free for further inactivation of Ach.

Reversible Anticholinesterases: - These are structurally similar to Ach & combine with Anionic & esteratic sites of cholinesterase as well as with Ach receptor. However the complex with esteratic site is much readily hydrolysed compared to Ach. This produces temporary inhibition of the enzyme.

Uses – Glaucoma, Myasthenia gravis, Snake venomPoisonimg, Curare Poisoning& Alzhmeir's disease.

Ir-reversible: - These organophosphorous compounds combine only with esteratic site of cholinesterase & consequently esteratic site is phosphorylated. The hydrolysis of esteratic site is extremely slow / does not occur at all.

This will lead to Morbidity & Mortality, to overcome this we use cholinesterase reactivators like Pralidoxime, Diacetylmonoxime&Obidoxime chloride.

Note: - Edrophonium forms reversible complex only with Anionic site & Hence shorter duration of action.

Echothiopate forms complex with both Anionic & esteratic sites & hence is much more potent than other compounds.

ANTI-CHOLINERGIC DRUGS

They Block only Muscarinic actions but not the Ganglionic & skeletal neuromuscular actions of Ach.

Classification:-

1. Natural alkaloids – Atropine, Scopalamine

2. Semisynthetic derivatives – Homatropine, Ipatropium

3. Synthetic compounds – a) Mydriatics: - Cyclopentolate, Tropicamide

   B) Antisecretory: - Propantheine, Pirenzepine

MOA: - Belladonna alkaloids block muscarinic effects of Ach. The antagonism is of competitive type which is reversed by an increase in Ach concentration at the cholinergic nerve endings

P.actions:- Atropine & scopolamine have qualitatively similar actions except that Atropine is CNS stimulant While Scopalamine is CNS Depressant.

1. **Secretions** – Decreases gastric secretions including total acidity & enzymes, leading to decreased motility

Decreases Nasal, Bronchial & other secretions

2. **Smooth muscles** – Relaxation, Causes Urinary retention

3. **Eye** - Mydriatic (1%), ciliary smooth muscle is paralyzed& produces tightening of suspensory ligament resulting in flattening of lens with consequent increase in focal length. Thus individual is able to see only at long distance (paralysis of accommodation/cycloplegia) Because of sphincter

paralysis he cannot constrict the pupils for viewing near objects clearly in response to Bright light (Photophobia).

4.   **CNS** – Atropine due to stimulation of medullary vagal nuclei & higher cerebral centers produces bradycardia, increase rate & depth of respiration produced by Anticholinesterases. Scopolamine by S.C.depresses RAS & Produces euphoria, Amnesia & dreamless sleep.

Therapeutic uses:-

- To control hypermotility, Colicky pain

- Organophosphorous compound poisoning

- As Antisecretory in Pre anaesthetic medication, Peptic ulcer& pulmonary embolism

- Motion sickness (scopolamine)

- Parkinsonism

- As Mydriatic& cycloplegic

- As Antispasmodic in   drug induced diarrhoea,

Spastic constipation, Gastritis&Dysmenorrhoea.

Contraindications:-

- May cause Congestive glaucoma in patients over 40yrs

- CCF with tachycardia

- Pyloric obstruction, pylorospasm&Cardiospasm

Ganglionic Stimulants: -

1. Nicotine, lobeline

2. Synthetic compounds (TMA, DMPP)

   Activation of Nicotinic receptors facilitate the release of Ach, NA, dopamine, 5-HT & **b** Endorphin

- Nicotine releases GH, Prolactin & ACTH

- Increases muscle twitching followed by paralysis of myoneuronal transmission

- Induces Hepatic microsomal enzymes

- Increases BMR, reduces body weight & Appetite

- Causes lipolysis & releases free fatty acids Excessive release of cortisol affect mood & contribute to Osteoporosis

- Vomitting due to action on CTZ, releases ADH by stimulating Supraoptic nuclei of Hypothalamus

  - Acidic urine Increases excretion of free nicotine, TMA & DMPP are excreted unchanged

  - A.R:- Bronchitis, Emphysema, Tobacco Amlobia

Cigarette contains – Nicotine, Pyridine.CO, Furfural, Volatile acids& polycyclic hydrocarbons Antidepressant like Bupropion is used to quit smoking in some individuals.

Note: - Mydriatics – Homatropine, Eucatropine & cyclopentolate

Other Antimuscarinics – Atropine methanitrate, Methoscopalmine bromide/Nitrates Propantheline (probanthine) – used in peptic ulcer Methantheline (Banthine), Dicyclomine

Pirenzepine (Gastrozepin) – in duodenal ulcer

Flavoxate (Uripas) & Oxybutynine (Ditropan) – In Dysurea, In urinary frequencies Tolteridine – M_3 antagonist in Urinary incontinence.

Ganglionic Blocking agents: - Blocks transmission across Autonomic ganglia (Both sympathetic & Parasympathetic)

examethonium, trimethomine&Hexamylamine

Skeletal muscle relaxants: - Used to treat spasm/spasicity

- Spasm – Involuntary contraction of muscle or group of muscles usually accompanied by pain & limited function.

- Spasticity – due to increased skeletal muscle tone associated with decrease in skeletal muscle power due to damage to the corticonotoneuronic pathways as in CNS injury, cerebral palsy, stroke or Multiple sclerosis.

Classification:-

1. Drugs acting centrally – diazepam, Baclofen& Mephenesin

2. Drugs acting peripherally at NMJ –

a) Competitive Blockers: - D-TC,

b) Depolarization blockers: - Succinyl choline

c) Inhibitors of release of Ach from the motor nerve terminals: - Botulinum

Toxin – A & Antibiotics (Tetracycline& Aminoglycosides)

3. Drugs directly acting on Skeletal muscles: - Dantrolene

PHYSIOLOGY OF SKELETAL MUSCLE CONTRACTION:-

1.   Due to nerve action potential releases Ach from synaptic vesicles of motor nerve in to synaptic cleft in large quantities, While in absence of NAP Ach is released due to miniature end plate potential (MEPP) in small quantities.

2.   The released Ach binds to nicotinic receptors on the motor endplate resulting in Localised depolarization & development of End plate polarization (EPP). Depolarization is due to influx of Na^+ & Efflux of K^+ ions from motor endplate.

3.   When EPP is achieved the surround area of muscle fibre gets excited resulting in development of muscle action potential (MAP) which initiates contraction of a muscle as a result of release of ca^{2+} in to the Sarcoplasm.

4.   Ach is metabolized enabling repolarisation of motor endplate& muscle fibre membrane. This is achieved by reversal of ionic fluxes. The polarized muscle is now capable of responding to fresh nerve impulse.

<u>Skeletal muscle contraction can be blocked as follows –</u>

1. Blocking transmission of impulse across the motor nerve – local anaesthetics

2. Inhibit the synthesis of Ach in motor nerve – Hemicholinum

3. Inhibit the release of Ach – Botulinum Toxin-A & antibiotics (tetracyclines& Aminoglycosides)

4. Modifying the motor endplate so that it does not respond to Ach – dantrolene

   D-Tc: - dextrorotatory, quaternary ammonium alkaloid from Chondrodendron Tomentosum Relaxes smooth muscles, Releases Histamine On repeated Administration produces cumulative toxicity. Do not cross BBB & Placental Barrier. Di-Methyl Tubocurarine has slightly longer duration of action

   Other drugs: - Alcuranium Chloride- Similar to D-Tc

   Pancuranium & Atracuranium – 5 times more potent than D-Tc Vercuranium Similar to Pancuranium but duration of action is less.

Gallamine – Similar to D-TC, less potent completely excreted by Kidneys in Unchanged form.

DRUGS USED IN PARKINSONISM

Extra pyramidal motor disorder characterized by Rigidity, tremor & Akinesia. Here Dopamine level decreases (responsible for Akinesia) & Ach level increases (Rigidity, Tremor).

Pathology: - There is a degeneration of neurons in substantial nigra & Nigrostatial (Dopaminergic) Tract. The cause for this degeneration is due to the formation of free radical (Metabolism of Dopamine by MAO-B). In normal Protective mechanisms Free radical are quenched by glutathione & other protective mechanisms. If this fails the free radical will cause DNA damage.

A synthetic toxin n-methyl 4-phenyl tetrahydropyridine is responsible for damage to Nigrostatial tract.

CLASSIFICATION:-

A. Drugs acting on dopaminergic system:-

1. Precursors of dopamine – L-Dopa
2. Drugs inhibit Dopamine Metabolism – A) Mao inhibitors: - Selelegine

   B) Comt inhibitors:-Tolcapone& Entacapone
3. Drugs that release dopamine – Amantidine
4. Dopamine agonists – Bromocryptine, Lysuride, ropinrole, Pergolide, Pirebedil

B. Anticholinergics: - Trihexyphenidyl, Benzohexol, Benzatropine

C. Antihistaminics: - Promethazine

L-Dopa:-

➤ Pharmacologically inert, while its metabolite is active.

➤ Only 1% enters CNS, Most of the drugs get decarboxylated in GIT& liver

➤ It is excreted in urine partly unchanged& partly as Homovanilic acid.

➤ Gives Positive Comb's test even though hemolytic anemia is not reported.

➤ Blood urea nitrogen & SGOT show a transient rise.

Contraindications:-

➤ Pyridoxine accelerates Peripheral decarboxylation of L-DOPA.

➤ Reserpine & Phenothiazines block the effects of dopamine to which L-Dopa is converted.

➤ Methyldopa intensifies the adverse effects of L-Dopa.

➤ Anticholinergics increase the stay of L-dopa in stomach & increase its degradation & hence if needed must be taken 2hrs before taking L-Dopa.

Dopa decarboxylase inhibitors (DCI):-

➤ Pharmacologically inactive but on combined administration with L-Dopa they do not enter BBB But decreases peripheral decarboxylation Of L-Dopa E.g. Carbidopa, Benserazide

L-dopa – Carbidopa combination results in control of symptoms smoother, dose of L- dopa Can be reduced up to 75%, Pyridoxine does not antagonize the actions of L- Dopa.

Selelegine (Deprenyl):- Inhibits MAO-B (responsible for dopamine metabolism) L-dopa – Carbidopa – Selelegine combination must be avoided.

Note – MAO-A is responsible for Oxidative deamination of NA & 5-HT.

Amantidine: - Liberate dopamine from residual intact nerve endings & produces rapid response than L-Dopa.

Dopamine Agonists: - Crosses BBB & need not to be converted to active metabolite.

Causes nausea& severe neuropsychatric adverse effects.

<u>CENTRAL NERVOUS SYSTEM</u>

Drugs act on CNS in following ways:-

1.   They may act directly on neurons & modify neuronal functions.

2.   They may act reflexly by sending afferent impulses to the CNS via chemoreceptors, Baroreceptors & peripheral nerves.

3.   They may affect the nutrition & oxygen supply of the CNS by altering its Blood supply or affecting its metabolism.

Neurotransmitters: - Which stimulate/Inhibit the post synaptic neurons after a brief latency & have short duration of action.

Amines – Ach, NA, 5-HT, Histamine& Dopamine

Aminoacids – l-Glutamic acid, Aspartic acid, GABA &Glycine Peptides – Substance-P, Cholecytokinin

Note: - Glutamate & Aspartate are excitatory amino acids. While GABA is inhibitory aminoacid.

Neuromodulators: - which act on the post synaptic neurons with a longer latency, have a longer duration of action & modify the responsiveness of the target neurons to the action of the neurotransmitters.

Aliphatic Alcohols:-

➢ Ethanol in 70% acts as antiseptic, in 40-50% as rubifacient & mild irritant action

➢ By dissolving in the lipid membrane of the neurons & altering the functions of ion channels & other proteins. It increases GABA-mediated synaptic inhibition. It also inhibits NMDA glutamate receptors. & depress CNS in descending order.

➢ Impairs Gluconeogenesis, Reduces synthesis of Albumin & Transferrin, Increases synthesis of VLDL with consequent Hypertriglyceredemia&Diminishes fatty acid oxidation.

➢ Alcohol causes liver damage & cause Cirrhosis. Elevated Gamma glutamyl transpeptidase (GGTP) is the most sensitive indication of Alcohol liver disease.

➢ Uses: - Appetizer, in methanol poisoning.

Treatment of Acute alcohol poisoning: - I.v glucose 50%,

I.v. Thiamine 100mg (Bolus), I.v. $MgSo_4$ 2-4gm

Treatment of Chronic alcoholism: - Disulfiram (Antabuse) & Citrated calcium cyanamide (Carbimide)

Disulfiram – It interferes with the oxidation of acetaldehyde formed during the metabolism of alcohol. It also inhibits dopamine-**b** Oxidase & thus interferes with the synthesis of NA. This causes depletion of catecholamines.

4-   Methyl pyrazole (inhibitor of alcohol dehydrogenase) used in treatment of methanol & ethylene glycol poisoning.

GENERAL ANAESTHETICS

They bring about loss of all Modalities of sensation in particularly pain along with a reversible loss of consciousness.

Minimum Alveolar concentration: - It is the minimum amount of the anaesthetic in pulmonary alveoli required to produce immobility in response to a painful stimuli, used in dose fixation& Capacity of anaesthetic is measured.

Classification:- A.Inhalational Anaesthetics –

1. Volatile liquids:-Chloroform, Diethyl ether, Trichloroethylene, Halothane, Enflurane & Isoflurane

2. Gases: - Cyclopropane, Nitrous oxide, chloroform & Cyclopropane

B. Non – volatile (I.v.) Anaesthetics –

1. Inducing agents: - Thiopentone sodium, Propafol, Etomidate

2. Slower acting drugs: - a) Benzodiazepines – Diazepam, Lorazepam&Midazolam

b) Dissociative Anaesthetics: - Ketamine

c) Neurolept Analgesia: - Fentanyl + Droperdiol (Analgesic)   (Butyrophenone)

M.O.A.:- Most of the general anaesthetics acts by blocking synaptic transmission but some act by blocking excitatory transmission but some act by prolonging the synaptic inhibition (Potentiaion of GABA-A) thus depressing all the functional elements of CNS. Inhalational anaesthetics, Barbiturates & Benzodiazepines act by potentiating the action of the inhibitory neurotransmitter GABA at $GABA_A$ receptor. Ketamine selectively inhibits the excitatory NMDA type of glutamate receptor.

Stages of Analgesia:-

1. Stage of analgesia – Minor surgical procedures such as incision of Abcess, dental extraction

Are carried successfully in this stage.

2. Stage of delirium – must be avoided.

3. Stage of surgical anaesthesia – Includes 4 Planes.

4. Stage of respiratory Paralysis –

Pre-Anaesthetic medication: - Term applied to the use of drugs prior to the administration of an anaesthetic agent, with the objective of making anaesthesia safer & more agreeable to the patient.

1.   Opoid analgesics – Morphine, Pethidine, Buprenorphine to reduce anxiety & apprehension of the patient.

2.   Sedative & Tranquilizers – Benzodiazepines& Barbiturates

3.   Anticholinergics – Atropine or Scopalamine

4.   Antiemetics – Phenothiazines(Promethazine & trimeprazine), Metoclopramide

5. H_2 Blockers – Ranitidine & famotidine to avoid gastric regurgitation & aspiration pneumonia

6.   Neuroleptics – Cpz, triflupromazine

Alphaxolone is a steroidal drug having anaesthetic property.

SEDATIVE & HYPNOTICS

Sedative reduces excitement & is commonly used as an Anxiolytic Hypnotic produces sleep resembling natural sleep.

CLASSIFICATION:-

1. **Barbiturates** – Long acting (Phenobarbitone & mephobarbitone)
   Short acting (Butobarbitone, Secobarbitone, and Pentobarbitone) Ultra short acting (Thiopentone, Methohexitone& Hexobarbitone)

2. **Benzodiazepines** – Anticonvulsant (Diazepam, Clonazepam& Clobazepam)
   Antianxiety (Diazepam, oxazepam, lorazepam, alprazolam, Chlordiazepoxide) Hypnotics (Diazepam, nitrazepam, flurazepam, temazepam, midazolam)

3. **Alcohols** – chloralhydrate, Ethchlorvynol

4. **Aldehydes** – Paraldehyde

5. **Acetylated carbinols** – Ethinamate, Meprobamate

6. **Imidazopyridine** – zolpidem

7. **Cyclopyralone** – Zopiclone

8. **Oxazolidine Diones** – Paramethadione & Trimethadione

9. **Miscellaneous** – Methaqualone, antihistaminics & scopolamine

M.O.A.:-

Barbiturates – They act primarily at the GABA: BZD receptor – Cl⁻ channel complex & they potentiate GABAergic inhibition by inducing the opening of the chloride channel.

Benzodiazepines – They act by enhancing presynaptic/postsynaptic inhibition through a specific BZD receptor, which is an integral part of the $GABA_A$ receptor – Cl⁻ channel complex. The binding site for GABA is located in the **b** subunit while the **a** subunit contains the BZD binding site. The modulatory BZD receptor increases the frequency of cl⁻ channel opening.

DRUGS AFFECTING $GABA_A$ RECEPTOR- CL⁻ CHANNEL COMPLEX ARE

	$GABA_A$	$GABA_B$	BZD site(a site)
Endogenous agonist	GABA	GABA	
Agonist	Muscimol	Baclofen	BZD
Competitive antagonist	Bicculine	Saclofen	Flumenazil
Inverse agonist			**b** carboline

ANTI – CONVULSANTS

These are the agents used to treat convulsions

Agents that produce convulsions are Bicculine, Pentylene tetrazole, Strychnine& Picrotoxin

CLASSIFICATION:-

1. Hydantoin derivatives – Phenytoin,Methatoin & ethatoin
2. Barbiturates – Phenobarbitone & Primidone
3. Iminostilbines – Carbamazepine
4. Succinimides – Ethosuximide & Methsuximide
5. GABA Transaminase inhibitors – Sodium Valproate, Vigabatrin

6.   GABA reuptake inhibitors – Tiagabin

7.   GABA Agonists – Gabapentin

8.   Benzodiazepines – Diazepam,Clonazepam&Clobazepam

9.   Miscellaneous–

Lamotrigine,Acetazolamide,Sultiame(Sulphonamide), Amphetamine

1. Hydantoin derivatives:-

M.O.A. – It acts by inhibiting the spread of seizure discharges in the Brain & Shortens the duration of after discharge. The drug causes dose-dependent block of sodium channels, thus reducing the neuronal sodium concentration leading to a reduction in Post titanic potentiation (PTP) & to increase the neuronal Potassium concentration.

AR – Hyperplasia, Hypertropy of gums, Osteomalacia, Hyperosmolar&non-Ketotic Coma. Uses – Grandmal, Focal cortical epilepsy. Psychomotor seizures & Neuralgia

2. Barbiturates;-

M.O.A. – Potentiates GABAergic inhibition

AR – Vit-K depletion, Megaloblastic Anaemia & osteomalacia

USE: They are used in the treatment of resistant grandmal, cortical seizures.

Primidone is a Deoxy Barbiturate converted in the liver to 2 active metabolites Phenobarbitone & Phenyl ethyl malonamide.

3. Iminostilbines: - It increases threshold to PTZ & Electroshock convulsions

AR – Peripheral neuritis, Agranulocytosis, Obstructive jaundice, Aplastic anaemia & Thrombocytosis, Diplopia, Vertiga, Ataxia & Lupus like Syndrome.

Uses – Temporal lobe & Grandmal epilepsy, Trigeminal neuralgia, Diabetes insipidus & Alternative to Lithium CO_3 in Mania.

4. Succinimides: - It acts by suppressing T-Current

AR – Blood dyscrasiasis, SLE, Psychic disturbances & GIT disturbances. Used in Temporal lobe epilepsy

5. **GABA transaminase Inhibitors: -** Potentiates Post synaptic GABA activity & decrease brain levels of EAA.

6. Oxazolidine Diones: - Raises threshold to Seizures

AR – Hemeralopia, Kidney damage **Used** in Petitmal epilepsy

7. **Miscellaneous:-**

Lamotrigine – blocks voltage sensitive sodium channel

Acetazolamide – Inhibits CA & acts by increasing CO_2 levels in the Brain or by decreasing sodium there by increasing Seizure threshold.

ANTIPSYCHOTICS

Antipsychotics/ Tranquilizers/ Ataractics are the drugs reduce Apomorphine induced Sterotype & Amphetamine induced Hyperactivity & also inhibit conditional avoidance response and cause some Ataxia.

CLASSIFICATION:-

1. Phenothiazine derivatives –

a) Aliphatic side chain: - CPZ, triflupromazine

b) Piperidine side chain: - Thioridazine & Mesoridazine

c) Piperazine side chain: - trifluperazine, Fluphenazine&thioproperazine

2. Butyrophenones – Haloperidol, Trifluperidol, Droperdiol&Penfluridol

3. Rauwolfia Alkaloids – Reserpine

4. Thioxanthines – Chlorprethixene, Thiothixene& Flupenthixol

5. Indole derivatives – Molindone

6. Substituted Benzamides – Sulpiride

7. Atypical neuroleptics – Clozapine (Dibenzodiazepines), Reserpidone

8. Miscellaneous – Oxypertine, Loxapine, Pimozide

Most of them act by following 3 ways-

1. Cause Blockade mainly of post synaptic Dopaminergic (D_2) receptors & to a small extent 5-HT receptors.
2. Modify functions of Mesolimbic system.
3. Reduce incoming sensory stimuli by acting on the brain stem reticular formation.

All Antipsychotics except clozapine have potent Dopamine (D_2) blocking action.

Dopamine acts as an excitatory neurotransmitter at D_1 & D_5 while Dopamine acts as an inhibitory neurotransmitter at D_2 , D_3& D_4 receptors.

Clozapine acts by 5-HT$_2$ as well as **a**1 Blockade. Reserpidone acts by 5-HT$_2$ as well as D_2 Blockade.

AR- Anticholinergic effect, Extrapyrimidal effects, Weight gain

<u>ANTI-ANXIETY AGENTS</u>

Elevated plus Maze test is used to evaluate Anti-anxiety agents.

Class	Drugs	M.O.A.
Benzodiazepines	Diazepam,Alprozolam,Oxazepam, Lorazepam,Chlordiazepoxide	Potentiates GABAergic Inhibition.
Azapirone	Buspirone,Gepirone,Ipsapirone	Stimulates Presynaptic 5-HT$_{1A}$ Autoreceptors.
Others	Meprobamate,Hydroxyzine	Antihistaminic with sedative, antimuscarinic & Spasmolytic actions.
b- blockers	Propranolol	By reducing B.p. tremor & palpitation.

AFFECTIVE DISORDERS

Refers to pathological change in mood state. The 2 Extremes are Mania & Depression. Drugs like Antidepressants & Antimanics (Mood stabilizers) are used.

Anti-Depressants:- A.MAO Inhibitors

1. Non-selective

a) Hydrazines: -   Phenelzine,   Isocarboxazid&   iproniazid

      Irreversible

   B) Non-Hydrazine:- Tranylcypromine

   c) Reversible: - Moclobemide

2. Isoenzyme Selective

a) MAO-A Inhibitor: - Clorgiline, Moclobemide

b) MAO-B Inhibitor: - Selelegine (Deprenyl)

B. Tricyclic Antidepressants

1. Nor-Adrenaline & 5-HT reuptake Inhibitors

   Imipramine, Amitryptiline, Trimipramine, Doxepin, Clomipramine, Dothiepin & Venlaflexin

2. Nor-Adrenaline reuptake Inhibitors

   Nortryptyline, Desipramine, Protryptiline, Amoxapine

3. Selective 5-HT reuptake Inhibitors

   Fluoxetine, Fluvoxamine, Paroxetine, sertraline & Alpacrolate

4. Atypical Antidepressants

   Trazodone, Bupropion, Mianserin, Tianeptine

   M.O.A:-

   MAO Inhibitors act by inhibiting MAO (Enzyme responsible for degradation of Catecholamines). Tricyclic Antidepressants Inhibit active uptake of Biogenic amines NA & 5-HT in to their respective neurons & thus potentiate them.

<u>ANTIMANICS/ MOOD STABILIZING DRUGS:-</u>

Lithium carbonate – They act by replacing Na^+ by Li^+ this affects ionic fluxes across Brain cells or modify the property of cellular membranes.

They decrease the release of NA & dopamine in the Brain with out affecting 5-HT release. They inhibit action of ADH on distal tubules & causes diabetes insipidus like state.

Alternatives used as Antimanics – Carbamazepine, Sodium valproate.

Hallucinogens: - (Psychomimetics/ Psychedelics/ Psychodysleptics/ Psychotogens)

These drugs alter mood, behavior, thought & perception in a manner similar to that seen in Psychosis.

Classification:-

1. **Indole amines:** - LSD, Psilocybin, Harmine, Bufotenine & dimethyltyrptamine

2. **Phenyl alkylamines: -** Mescaline

3. **ArylcycloHexylamines: -** Phencyclidine

4. **Cannabinoids: -** Tetrahydro Cannabinol

   Phencyclidine is a Hallucinogen structurally similar to Ketamine.

   Psychomotor stimulants: -

   Caffeine, Amphetamine & Piperidyl derivatives (Pipradrol & Methyl phenidate). Used in Narcolepsy, Catoplexy & Attention deficit Hyperactivity disorder (ADHD).

OPIOID ANALGESICS

☐ The opioid drugs produce their effects by combining with opioid receptors which are widely distributed in CNS & other tissues.

☐ Opiods & their Antagonists act at Mu receptors.

☐ The side effects such as vomiting, Sweating & Hallucinations are due to action of drugs on subtype of Kappa receptors.

	M	j	K
Endogenous Agonists	Endomorphin 1&2 b-Endorphin (31a.a)	Leu/Meth Enkephalein (5a.a)	Dynorphin A
Exogenous agonists	Morphine	Morphine	Ketocyclazocine
Selective agonists	b-Funaltrexamine m_1-naloxanazine		Norbinaltorphimine

Opium alkaloids are divided as

1. Phenanthrene group

2. Benzyl isoquinoline – Papaverine, Noscapine

Devoid of analgesic activity, Intracarvenosal injection of papaverin causes penile errection. Noscapine is a potent releaser of Histamine. & large doses cause Hypotension.

Morphine – Used as sulfate/HCl salt

Produces Analgesia, Euphoria, sedation& Hypnosis.

Causes direct depressant action on Brain stem respiratory centre & reduce the sensitivity of medullary respiratory centre to increased plasma CO_2 concentration. With toxic doses breathing is entirely maintained by 'Hypoxic Drive' mediated through the carotid & aortic body chemoreceptors & results in 'Cheyne Stokes Respiration'.

Causes Miosis, Nausea Cough suppression, Stimulates Vagus nuclei, Excites spinal cord & raises CSF.It also releases ADH.

GIT: - spasms followed by increase in intrabiliary pressure.

T.uses – Powerful analgesic, sedative, Pre-anaesthetic medication, general anaesthetic Contraindications- In, hypopitutarism, Addison's disease, Head injuries, impaired kidney & liver functions.

Codeine – Devoid of respiratory depression, enhances analgesic effect in combination with Aspirin.

Note: - All the 3 types of receptors are antagonized by Opioid antagonists such as Naloxone & Naltrexone.

The drugs which act as partial agonist-antagonists at the opioid receptors are Nalorphine, Levallorphan, and Pentazocine&Nalbuphine.

NSAIDS: - Extensively protein bound drugs.

Classification –

1. Salicylates:-

2. p-Aminophenol derivatives: - Phenacetin, Paracetamol, & Acetanilide

3. Pyrazolone derivatives: - Phenyl Butazone

4. Indole & related drugs: - Indomethacin, Sulindac

5. Heterocyclic Aryl acetic acid derivatives: - Diclofenac, Tolmetin&Keterolac

6. Propionic acid derivatives: - Ibuprofen, fenoprofen, Naproxen, Ketoprofen

7. Fenamates: - Flufenamic acid, & Mefenamic acid

8. Oxicams: - piroxicam

9. Sulfonanilides: - Nimesulide

:- Cox-1 is present in Stomach, Kidney& Blood vessels. Where as Cox-2 in inflammatory cells& activated leucocytes.NSAIDS act by inhibiting COX, responsible for the conversion of arachidonic acid to Prostaglandins.

Salicylates: - prevent the release of Histamine, Lowers ESR (erythrocyte sedimentation rate) Inhibits platelet aggregation. In small doses elevate plasma urate levels while in large doses causes uricosuria. Induces release of adrenaline from adrenal medulla.

In case of salicylate poisoning supplement of Vit-k is given along with other formalities. Trusses – Antirheumatic,

Antiplatelet, Analgesic, Antipyretic, Counterirritant, Keratolytic, fungistatic, Antiseptic, Antiinflammatory.

Selective Cox-2 inhibitors: - Nimesulide, celecoxib, rofecoxib, meloxicam

GASTROINTESTINAL DRUGS

Achlorhydria: - Absence in production of HCL leading to improper digestion. It can be treated by 10ml of 10% HCL diluted 100ml H_2O.

Hypochlorhydria: - decreased production of HCL.

Sialorrhoea: - increased salivary production

ORS: - Oral rehydration solution. Glucose – 20g, Nacl – 3.5g, Kcl – 1.5g, $NaHCo_3$ (2.5g) or tri sodium citrate (2.9g) – distilled water (1-L).

Mumps: - infectious, inflammatory swelling of paratoid & salivary glands.

Hydragogue: - Drug which produces watery stools.

Dyspepsia: - disorder of abdomen or chest with flatulence, nausea etc.

Achyliagestrica: - Absence of HCL.

Bitters: - They increase appetite by promoting gastric acid secretion. E.g.:- gentian, chirata, picrorrhiza Alcohol & 2 other Antihistaminics (cyproheptidine, Buclizine) also acts as appetite stimulants.

Anorexia nervosa: - Chronic disease characterized by loss of appetite, weight loss, physiological & psychological alterations.

Digestants: - which aid in digestion in GIT. E.g.:- Diastase & Taka diastase – Amylolytic,

Papain – Proteolytic,

Pancreatin – Amylolytic & Proteolytic, Bromelain – Amylolytic, lipolytic & proteolytic, Lipase – Lipolytic.

Carminatives: - expels gas with relaxation of sphincters. E.g.:- Volatile oils & Spices.

Gall stone dissolving drugs: - Ursodiol & chenodiol

Bile salts are essential for digestion of cholesterol, when the amount of cholesterol in body increases, they form gall stones, and thereby bile acids are used for dissolving gall stones.

Bile acids: - Chenodiol (cholic acid) & Ursodiol (taurocholic acid) both inhibit absorption of cholesterol.

Bile salts: - Sodium glycocholate & sodium taurocholate.

Bile pigments: - Bilurubin, Biliverdin, Stercobilin & Stercobilinogen.

Peptic ulcer: - due to imbalance between aggressive factors (acid, pepsin & H-pylori) & defensive factors (gastric mucus & bicarbonate secretions, PG'S innate resistance of the mucosal cells).

METHODS OF TREATING PEPTIC ULCER:-

1. **By reducing gastric acid secretion :-**

Class	Drugs	M.O.A	A.R.
H2 Blockers	Cimetidine ranitidine Roxatidine Famotidine	Blacks H2 receptors	Cimetidine causes gynacomastia & inhibiting cytp450
Proton pump inhibitors	Omeprazole Lansoprazole Pantoprazole	H+K+ inhibits Atpase present in parietal cells	Nausea headache loose stools

Anticholinergies	pirenzepine Propantheline	Decreases cholinergic secretions	Intolerable side effects
PG Analogues	Misoprostol Rioprostil Enprostil	Inhibit acid secretion & promote mucus & bicarbonate secretion Inhibit gastrin production	Contraindicated in pregnancy

Cimetidine Produces Anti Androgen Effect by displacing the Dihydro testosterone from the cytoplasmic receptors, Increases plasma prolactin level & inhibits the metabolism of Estrogens.

2. **Neutralization of gastric acid:** - Systemic antacids – $NaHco3$, Non Systemic antacids – $Al (oH)_3$, $Mg (oH)_2$.

    MAGALDRATE – Hydrated complex of Hydroxy Magnesium Aluminate.

    Acid neutralizing capacity: - Number of milli equivalents of 1N HCL that is brought to PH

    3.5 in 15 mins by unit dose of the preparation.

3. **Ulcer protectives :-**

    Sucralfate – Aluminium salt of sulfated sucrose at pH – 4 it polymerizes to form a gel & gets deposited on the wall of stomach.

    Colloidal Bismuth Sub citrate – increases Pg synthesis. They also destroy H.Pylori

4. **Ulcer healing drugs:** - Carbenoxolone sodium, Deglycyrrhizinised licorice.

5. **Anti.H.Pylori:-** Metronidazole, Tinidazole.

    Combination therapy = Clarithromycin + Amoxycillin + Omeprazole.

    Polymethyl siloxane: - Collapes froth, improves dispersion of Antacid, reduces gastro esophageal reflux & thus relieves Heart Burn.

    Drug contraindicated in peptic ulcer: Caffeine, reserpine, Aminophylline, glucocorticoids, NSAIDS.

    EMETICS

    Emetine, Apomorphine, Hypertonic saline solution, mustard (sinigrin)

    Anti emetics:-

    Anticholinergies – Hyoscine, Dicyclomine

H$_1$ Antihistaminics – Promethazine, Diphenhydramine, Cyclizine, Cinnarazine

Neuroleptics – CPZ, Haloperidol, Prochlorperazine **Prokinetic drugs** – Metoclopramide, Domperidone, **5HT$_3$ antagonists** – Ondansetron, granisetron

DRUGS ACTING ON RESPIRATORY SYSTEM

Respiratory quotient: - ratio of oxygen consumed to the carbondioxide evolved.

1. **Pharyngeal demulcents: -** sooth the throat directly as well as by promoting salivation E.g.:- Lozenges, Glycerine, Liquorice.

2. **Expectorants (mucokinetics):-**

   Directly acting:- eucalyptus & lemon oil, Guainaphenesin, Vasaka.

3. **Reflexly acting: -** saline expectorants (NH4cl, KI, K-citrate)

4. **Antitussives :-**

   ☐ Opioids – Codeine, morphine.

   ☐ Non-Opioids – Noscapine, Dextrometrorphan, Clophedianol, Carbetopentane & Oxeladin

5. **Antihistaminics –** Chlorpheniramine, diphenhydramine, Promethazine

6. **Mucolytic agents: -** decreases viscosity of sputum. E.g.:- Acetylcysteine, bromohexine, Ambroxol pancreatic dornase.

7. **Nasal decongestants:** - ephedrine, phenyl ephrine Naphazoline & Oxymetazoline.

   Bronchodilators:-

1. **Sympathominetics** – ephedrine, adrenaline, salmeterol

2. **Methyl xanthines** – Theophylline

3. **Anticholinergics** – Ipratropium bromide Atropine methonitrate.

   ☐ Cromolyn sodium is a prophylactic agent that stabilizes most cells in asthma.

   ☐ Prednisolone is life saving in serve status asthamaticus & inhibitor of phospholipase A$_2$.

   ☐ Ipratropium is bronchodilator in chronic obstructive pulmonary disease with least cardiac effects.

- Ketotifen – Orally active, Prophylactic agent in Bronchial Asthma & Allergic disorders.

  - Inhalational Steroids – Beclomethasone, dipropionate& Budesonide.

DRUGS ACTING ON C.V.S

Cardiac glycosides: - These glycosides have cardiac inotropic activity. They increase myocardial contractility & output without proportionate increase in O_2 consumption. E.g.:- Digitoxin, Digoxin, Lanatoside – C, quabain

M.O.A:- Cardiac glycosides selectively bind to membrane bound Na^+/K^+ ATPase pump. This results in accumulation of Na^+ intracellularly and this indirectly results in intracellular accumulation of $Ca2^+$, this leads to increased myocardial contractility.

Therapeutic index = 1.5 – 3.0 (Digitalis)

Properties	Digitoxin	Digoxin	Lanatoride – c	Quabain
Oral absorption	Excellent	Good	Low	Low
PPB	95 %	25%	25%	Poor
2plasma t1/2	7 days	2 days	2 days	1 day
Potency	Less	Intermediate	Intermediate	High
Elimination	Hepatic	Renal	Renal	Renal

Uses: - CCF, cardiac arrhytmias such as atrial flutter & atrial fibrillation.

Cardiac arrhythmias: - refers to changes in Cardiac rhythm.

Antiarrhythmic drugs:-

I – Sodium channel Blockers

Class	M.O.A	Examples
IA	Prolongs repolarisation	Quinidine, Procainamide Disopyramide.
IB	Shortens repolarisation	Lidocaine, Phenytoin tocainide.
IC	Slows conduction	Encainide, Flecainide Propafenone.

Affinity towards Na+channel = class IC > class IA > class IB

II – B Blockers E.g.:- propranalol

<u>M.O.A</u>:- slows conduction & suppresses automaticity.

III – K+ channel blocker E.g.:- Amiadarone, Bretylium, Sotalol

<u>M.O.A</u>:- prolongs refraction

IV – ca2+ channel blocker E.g.:- verpamil, Diltiazem blocks inward ca2+ current. V – Digitalis.

Cardiac arrhythmic disorders	First line drugs/ Drug of choise
PSVT	Adenosine/Verpamil
Av Block	Atropine
Atrial extra systole	Quinidine
Atrial flutter/Atrial fibrillation	Verapamil
Ventricular extra systole/ventricular tachycardia	Lidocaine
Wolf Parkinson white syndrome	Amiodarone/Flecainide

ANTI-ANGINAL DRUGS

Used to treat Angina pectoris

<u>Angina pectoris:</u> - where the O_2 demand of the myocardium exceeds that of the supply.

<u>Stable angina:</u> - generally caused due to stress

<u>Unstable angina:</u> - due to occlusion of coronary arteries by plague.

<u>Variant / Prinzmetal angina:</u> - It occurs at rest due to recurrent localized coronary vasospasms.

Classification:-

A. **<u>Organic nitrates:</u>** - i) <u>sh</u>ort acting: - glyceryl trinitrate.

ii) Long acting: - ISDN, ISMN.

B. **<u>B – Blockers:</u>** - Propranalol.

C. **<u>$Ca2^+$ channel Blockers:</u>** - Verapamil, Nifedepine, Diltiazem.

D. **<u>K^+ channel openers:</u>** - Nicorandil, minoxidil.

E. **<u>Antiplatelet drugs:</u>** - Aspirin, Dipyridamole.

F. **<u>Cytoprotectives:</u>** - Trimetazidine.

- L-arginine   N.O.synthetase   N.O. +citrulline
- Organic nitrates are rapidly denitrated in the smooth muscle cell to release the reactive free radical N.O. that activates guanyl cyclase, which causes the formation of CGMP from GTP. CGMP causes desphorphorylation of MLCK through CGMP dependent proteinkinase. Reduced availability of phosphorylated MLCK interferes with activation of myosin & it fails to interact with actin & this leads to relaxation.
- Nitrates are also used to treat cyanide poisoning as nitrates form methemoglobin with Hb. So that cyanide cannot act on methemoglobin.

Potassium channel openers: - since intracellular concn of K^+ is much higher compared to extra cellular region, K+ channel opening results in outflow of K^+ ions & hyperpolarisation. <u>Uses</u>: - Angina pectoris, Hypertension, CHF. <u>AR</u>: - Hirsutism.

Desferrioxamine: - A high affinity iron cheater used as a protective in ischemic myocardial injury through its anti-free radical effect.

Vasodilators: - They are used in Hypertension, myocardial infarction, angina attacks etc.

1) Arteriolar vasodilators: - Hydralazine, minoxidil, nifedepine, diazoxide, nicorandil.
2) Venous vasodilators: - Glyceryl trinitrate, ISDN.
3) Mixed vasodilators: - Losartan, sodium nitroprusside, prazosin.

Selective phosphodiesterase inhibitor: - Amrinone is an inotropic agent. It is a bipyridine derivative & inhibits PDE – III.

Milrinone (derivative of Amrinone) & 10 times more potent than Amrinone. Drotavarin inhibits PDE – V.

Non-selective PD inhibitor: - Cilastazole & Theophylline dithiothreol is used to stop the action of nitrates by removing nitrate groups attached to 'SH'.

<u>ANTIHYPERTENSIVE DRUGS</u>:

- These are drugs used to lower BP in Hypertension.
- Blood pressure is the product of cardiac output and peripheral resistance.

- Cardiac output is the amount of blood pumped by the heart in one minute and is therefore the product of stroke volume and the heart rate. Stroke volume refers to the volume of blood pumped during each contraction.

  - B.P = C.O * T.P.R, C.O = stroke volume * Heart rate.

- Thus it can be observed that most of the antihypertensive drugs act by either decreasing peripheral resistance or by decreasing cardiac output.

CLASS	DRUGS	MECHANISM OF ACTION MOA	ADVERSE EFFECTS
ACE inhibitor	Enalpril, (prodrug) Lisinorpril, (prodrug) Ramipril (prodrug) Captopril (nonprodrug) Saralasin	They inhibit ACE essential for the conversion of AT-I to AT- II, which is a potent vasoconstrictor	Dry cough, angioedema, Urticaria and taste disturbance.
Angiotensin receptor antagonist	Losartan, irbesatran valsartan, telmisatran candesartan (Peptide analogue).	They antagonize the action of AT-II at the angiotensin receptor.	Usually well tolerated.
Calcium channel blockers	Verapamil, nifedepine, amlodipine	They lower b.p by decreasing peripheral resistance	Agents such as diltiazem/verapamil have negative inotropic action.
Diuretics	Chlorthiazide, furosemide, spironolactone.	They induce diuresis that reduces plasma volume which in turn reduces C.O leading to a drop in b.p.	Thiazide diuretics cause hypokalemia and also hyperglycemia in diabetics.
- Blockers	Metoprolol, propranolol	They decrease sinus rhythm, which leads to a decrease in heart rate, which leads to a drop in b.p.	Myocardial insufficiency Bradycardia Asthma Heart block. Insulin dependent diabetics.

☐ **Adrenergic blockers**	Prazosin, terazosin	They block the action of adrenaline at the a receptor present in blood vessels thereby leading to vasodilatation	Impotence postural hypo tension
Central sympatholytics	Methyldopa clonidine (h2 agonist)	The-nor methyl adrenaline formed from methyldopa acts as false neuro transmitter on a2 and decreases efferent sympathetic activity.	Sedation, lethargy and reduced mental capacity.
Neurotransmitter depletors	Guanethedine reserpine	Displaces N.T. from synapse increases N.T.metabolism	
Vasodilators	Hydralazine, minoxidil	Vasodilatation leads to a decrease in peripheral resistance, which in turn leads to fall in b.p.	Hydralazine on prolonged use causes SLE (Systematic lupus erythrematosus), hirsustism, peripheral pooling of blood.

Ethacyranic acid is contraindicated in Angina in Asthma B2 blockers is avoided.

ANTIHYPERLIPIDEMIC DRUGS:

These drugs lower the levels of lipoproteins and lipids in blood. The different types of hyperlipoproteinemia are:

Type	Disorder	Elevated plasma lipoprotein	Elevated plasma lipids
I	Lipoprotein lipase deficiency	Chylomicron	Cholesterol & triglycerides
IIa	Familial hypercholesterolemia	LDL	Cholesterol
IIb	Polygenic hypercholesterolemia	LDL (B-lipoprotein)	Cholesterol (moderate increase)
III	Familial Dysbetalipoproteinemia	IDL, chylomicron remnants	Cholesterol & triglycerides
IV	Hypertriglycereridemia	VLDL (pre-B lipoprotein)	Triglycerides
V	Hyperlipedemia	VLDL, LDL	Cholesterol & triglycerides

THE CLASSIFICATION OF HYPOLIPEDEMIC DRUG IS AS FOLLOWS:

Class	Drugs	Mechanism of action	Adverse effects
HMG-CoA Reductase inhibitors	Lovastatin, atorvastatin, simvastatin	They inhibit the enzyme HMG-CoA Reductase essential for the conversion of HMG-CoA to mevalonate and thus inhibit synthesis of cholesterol.	Headache, rise in serum transaminase, rise in CPK levels.
Bile acid sequestrants	Cholestyramine, colestipol	These are ion exchange resins that bind bile acids in the intestine inhibit their enterohepatic circulation. Cholesterol is absorbed with the help of bile acids and in their absence, it is excreted.	Unpalatable and may cause nausea, flatulence, heartburn, constipation.
Fibric acid derivatives	Clofibrate, Gemfibrozil, fenofibrate	They activate lipoprotein lipase which is essential for the degradation VLDL resulting in lowering of TG's.	Increased appetite and weight gain, myalgia and increased incidence of gallstones.
Others	Neomycin, gugulipid probucol	Neomycin lowers LDL-CH by complexing with bile acids in the intestine. Guggul lipid probucol acts as Antioxidant	Neomycin may however damage intestinal mucosa. Loose stools.

☐ *Comniphora molmol* – myrh (antiseptic),

☐ *Comniphora mukul* – guggul (antihyperlipedemic).

☐ **Dromotropic** – Drug affects conductivity of impulses in neuronal cells.

HORMONES

➤ They are mediator molecules act as chemical messengers.

➤ They are released in one part of the body & regulates activity of cells in other ports of Body.

➤ Hormones are secreted by endocrine or ductless glands.

➤ Most hormones enter interstitial fluid & then the Bloodstream.

:- Hormones like, neurotransmitters, influence their target cells by chemically binding to specific protein or glycoprotein receptors.

SITE OF ACTION:-

At cell membrane receptors – E.g.:- Adrenaline, glucagons, FSH, LH, TSH, ACTH calcitonin, vasopressin, oxytocin, insulin etc.

At cytoplasmic receptors – E.g.:- steroidal Hormones.

At nuclear receptors – Thyroid Hormones.

Down regulation: - when hormone is present in excess, the no. of target cells receptors decreases. This makes target cells less responsive to the hormone.

Up regulation:- when there is a deficiency in hormone is the no. of receptors may increase. This makes target cells more sensitive to hormone

Classification of hormones: - The endocrine glands include pituitary, Thyroid, Parathyroid, Adrenal and pineal glands.

Water soluble hormones: - protein eicosanoid hormones.

Lipid soluble hormones: - Steroid, Thyroid & gaseous hormone (Nitric oxide). **Placental hormones: -** Chronic gonadotropin – Prolactin, Estrogens – Progesterone, **Placental lactogen** – Chorionic thyrotropin.

Hormones of the Anterior & Posterior Pituitary:-

Hormone	Secreted by	Releasing Hormone (stimulates secretion)	Inhibiting hormone (suppresses secretion)
Human growth hormone (hGH) or somatotropin (191aminoacid)	Somatotrophs	Growth hormone-releasing hormone (GHRH) or somatocrinin (44A.A)	Growth harmone- inhibiting hormone (GHIH) or somatostain (14AA)
Thyroid-stimulating hormone (TSH) or thyrotropin	Thyrotrophs	Thyrotropin releasing hormone (tripeptide)	Growth hormone- inhibiting hormone somatostatin
Follicle-stimulating harmone (FSH)	Gonadotrophs	Gonadotrophic releasing harmone(decapeptide)	---------
Luteinizing harmone (LH)	Gonadotrophs	Gonadotrophic releasing harmone	---------
Prolactin (PRL) (198aminoacid)	Lactotrophs	Prolactin releasing harmone	Prolactin inhibiting harmone or dopamine
Adrenocorticotropic harmone (ACTH) or corticotrophin	Corticotrophs	Corticotropin releasing harmone (41 aminoacids)	---------
Mealanocyte-stimulating harmone (191aminoacid)	Corticotrophs	Corticotropin releasing harmone	Dopamine

☐ Leuprolide is a synthetic non-peptide of GTRH.

☐ Dropamine antagonist not given in lactating women because it inhibits prolactin. Enuresis – Bed wetting (Desmopressin)

☐ Melatonin – (responsible for normal sleep)

☐ Posterior pituitary or neurohypophysis does not synthesize harmones; it stores and releases two harmones oxytocin and antidiuretic harmones (vasopressin).

HORMONE	PRINCIPAL ACTIONS
Human growth harmone (hGH) or somatotropin	Stimulates liver, muscle, cartilage, bone, and other tissues to synthesize and secrete insulin like growth factors. (IGF's); IGFs promote growth of body cells, protein synthesis, tissue repair, lipolysis, and elevation of blood glucose concentration.
Thyroid-stimulating harmone (TSH) Or Thyrotropin	Stimulates synthesis and secretion of thyroid harmones by thyroid gland
Follicle-stimulating harmone (FSH)	In females, initiates development of oocytes and induces ovarian secretion of estrogens. In males stimulates testes to produce sperm.
Luteinizing harmone (LH)	In females, stimulates secretion of estrogens and progesterone, ovulation and formulation of corpus luteum. In males, stimulates interstitial cells in testes to develop and produce testosterone.
Prolactin (PRL) more active in presence of oxytocin	Together with other harmones, promotes milk secretion by the mammary glands.
Adrenocorticotropic harmone (ACTH) or corticotrophin	Stimulates secretion of glucocorticoids (mainly coritsol) by adrenal cortex.
Melanocyte-stimulating harmone	Exact role in humans is unknown but may influence brain activity, when present in excess, can cause darkening of skin.
Oxytocin (OT)	Stimulates contraction of smooth muscle cells of uterus during childbirth; stimulates contraction of myoepithelial cells in mammary glands to cause milk ejection.
Antidiuretic harmone (ADH) or vasopressin	Conserves body water by decreasing urine volume; decreases water loss through perspiration; raises blood pressure by constricting arterioles.

<u>Pitutary harmone derivates:-</u>

	ANALOGUE	USES
Bromocriptine	Prolactin inhibitor	Cancer therapy
Desmopressin	ADH	Diabetes insipidus
Gasrelin, coryntropin, Leuprolide	ACTH	Infantile spasms
Menotropins, urofollitin	FSH, LH	Infertility
Naferelin	GNRH	Cancer, Infertility
Ocreolide	Somatostatin	Inhibits glandular

GONADAL HARMONES	USES
Tamoxifen	Breast cancer
Diethylstilbesterol	After contraception
Estrogen & progesterone	Oral contraception
Norgesterol & medroxyprogesterone	chronic contraception
Mifepristone	Abortifacient
Oxandralone	Anabolic

<u>THYROID GLAND</u>

The follicular cells produce two harmones; thyroxine (tetraiodothyronine) and tri- iodothyronine, which are known as thyroid harmones.

Synthesis and secretion of T3 and T4 occurs as follows:

a. <u>**Iodine trapping:**</u> Follicular cells trap iodine ions by an active transport mechanism.

b. <u>**Synthesis of thyroglobulin:**</u> While the follicular cells are trapping iodide ions, they are also producing thyroglobulin (TGB).

c. <u>**Oxidation of iodide:**</u> Iodine ions are oxidized by peroxidase to form iodine (I2).

d. <u>**Iodination of tyrosine:**</u> as iodine molecules form, they react with tyrosines that are part of thyroglobulin molecules. Binding of one iodine atom with tyrosine yields mono-iodotyrosine (T1), while two iodine atoms yields di-iodotyrosine (T2),

e. <u>**Coupling of T1 and T2**</u>: two T2 molecules combine to form T4 while one T1 and one T2 combine to form T3 in the presence of peroxidase.

<u>**Calcitonin: -**</u> It is a harmone produced by the parafollicular cells of the thyroid gland. It decreases the level of calcium in blood by inhibiting the action of osteoclasts, the cells that break down bone matrix.

<u>**Parathormone: -**</u> It is secreted by the parathyroid glands and it increases blood calcium and magnesium levels, while it decreases phosphate levels.

The harmones produced by the adrenal cortex are of three types:

a. Mineral corticoids : Aldosterone

b. Glucocorticoids: Cortisol, Coorticosterone & Cortisone.

c. Androgens: Dehydroepidandrosterone.

The harmones produced by the chromaffin cell of the adrenal medulla are Epinephrine and nor epinephrine.

The four types of pancreatic islets that produce harmones are:-

1. A cells secrete glucagons.

2. B cells secrete insulin.

3. D cells secrete somatostatin.

4. F cells secrete pancreatic polypeptide.

Hormone	Control of secretion	Principal actions
Thyroid harmone	Secretion is increased by thyrotopin-releasing harmone and high thyroid iodine levels suppresses secretion.	Increase basal metabolic rate, stimulate synthesis of proteins, and increase use of glucose.
Calcitonin	High blood calcium levels stimulates secretion, low levels suppresses secretion.	Lowers blood levels of ionic calcium and phosphate.
Parathyroid hormone	Low blood calcium levels stimulate secretion; High blood calcium levels inhibit secretion.	Increases blood calcium and magnesium levels and decreases phosphate levels.
Mineral corticoids	Increased blood K+ level and angiotensin II stimulates secretion.	Increases blood levels of Na+ and water and decrease blood level of K+.
Glucocorticoids	ACTH stimulates release.	Increase protein breakdown stimulate gluconeogenesis.
Androgens	ACTH stimulates release.	Assist in early growth of axillary and public hair.

Epinephrine and Nor epinephrine	Sympathetic preganglionic neurons release acetylcholine, which stimulates secretion.	Produce effects that enhance those of the sympathetic division of the automatic nervous system during stress.
Glucagon	Decreased blood level of glucose, exercise and mainly protein meals stimulate secretion.	Raises blood glucose level by accelerating breakdown of glycogen into glucose in liver.
Insulin	Increased blood level of glucose, acetylcholine, arginine and leucine, glucagon, GIP, hGH, and ACTH stimulate secretion.	Lowers blood glucose level by accelerating transport of glucose into cells, converting glucose into glycogen and stimulates protein synthesis.
Somatostatin	Pancreatic polypeptide inhibits secretion.	Inhibits secretion of insulin and glucagon and slows absorption of nutrients from the gastrointestinal tract.
Pancreatic polypeptide	Meals containing protein, fasting, exercise, and acute hypoglycemia stimulate secretion.	Inhibits somatostatin secretion, gallbladder contraction, and secretion of pancreatic digestive enzyme.

Hormones affecting calcium homeostasis:-

- Calciferol (25 Hydroxy Vit-D3)

- Calcitrol (1, 25 dihydroxy Vit-D3)

- Cholecalciferol (Vit-D3)

- Secalcifediol (24, 25 dihydroxy vitD3)

- Ergocalciferol (VitD2)

- **Androgens: -** Testosterone, Oxandrolone, Stanozolol.

- **Antiandrogens: -** Finasteride (synthetic inhibitors).

- **Antiprogestins: -** Mifepristone.

It deals with the use of chemical agent to arrest the progress of infectious diseases by destroying infective parasites or microbes without damaging the host tissues.

M.O.A:-

1. **INHIBITING PROTEIN SYNTHESIS BY BINDING TO RIBOSOMAL SUBUNIT & DESTROYING THE BACTERIAL CELL.**

   E.g.:- Gentamycin & streptomycin.

2. **REVERSIBLE INHIBITION OF PROTEIN SYNTHESIS BY ACTION ON RIBOSOME.**

   E.g.:- Broad spectrum Antibiotics

3. **BY DETERGENT ACTION (LEAKAGE OF CELL CONSTITUENTS)**

A. Direct cell membrane. E.g.:- Colistin, Polymyxin

B. Drug binding to cell wall sterols. E.g.:- Nystatin, Amphotercin.

4. **INHIBITION OF CELL WALL SYNTHESIS: -**

   E.g.:- Penicillins, Cephalosporins, sulphonamides.

5. **DRUGS AFFECTING NUCLEICACID METABOLISM:-**

A. Inhibition of DNA dependent RNA polymerase. E.g.:- Refampicin.

B. Inhibition of DNA supercoiling & DNA synthesis. E.g.:- Quinolones & Fluoroquinolones.

DRUG RESISTANCE:-

1. **Natural: -** Organisms do not have target sit for drugs to act. E.g.:- Antifungals in Bacterial infections.

2. **Acquired:** - Organisms are exposed to the drug in such a manner that it develops resistance.

Cross resistance: -

Development of resistance to one substance may also show resistance to another substance to which the organism has not been exposed. E.g.:- resistance between Sulphonamides, resistance between Tetracycline's, resistance between Tetracycline's & Chloramphenicol.

There is no cross resistance between Animoglycosides.

<u>**Super infection/Supra infection**</u>: -

➢ It is due to the use of Broad spectrum antibiotics.

➢ There is no. of microorganisms inhabiting GIT & these organisms constitute the microbial flora. They are called as "commensals" under normal conditions; these organisms compete with another for nutrients. & therefore they are unable to proliferate rapidly.

➢ When a Broad spectrum antibiotic such as chloramphenical / tetracycline is administered, it might kill most of the microbial flora barring a few organisms. Now these few microbes are free to proliferate rapidly in the absence of competition & they multiply, spread all over the body & cause infections called super infections.

<u>**Antimicrobial agent**</u>: - An agent which kills M.O. or suppresses their growth. The susceptibility of AMA is determined by

1. Radiometric method
2. Resistance ratio method (Traditional).

<u>**Sulfonamides & Sulfones**</u>

These are derived from prontosil red (dye) & are effective against pyogenic Bacterial Infections.

<u>**CLASSIFICATION**</u>:-

1. Short acting: - Sulfadiazine, Sulfisoxazole.
2. Intermediate: - Sulfamethoxazole.
3. Long acting: - Sulfadoxine, Sulfamethopyrazine.
4. In intestinal infections: - Sulfasalazine.
5. In Burn therapy: - Silver sulfadiazine, mafenide.
6. In ophthalmic infection: - Sulfacetamide.

Guanosine............> PABA____________>   Dihydropteroic acid

Several steps   (-) Sulfonamides (-) Trimethoprim <.............

____________________________Dihydrofolic acid folate reductase folic acid

DIHYDRO FOLATE REDUCTASE

➢ Tetrahydrofolic acid ------------------------ N5, N10 methylene FAH4
➢ N5formylFaH4 -----------------------N10 formyl FAH4

➤ N5formylFAH4, N5N10 methylene FAH4, N10formyl FAH4 is very essential for several Biosynthetic pathways in humans & Bacteria.

➤ The growth and cell division in bacteria can be stopped if any drug blocks Biosynthesis of folate co-enzymes.

➤ Folate co-enzymes are biosynthesized from dietary folic acid in humans & other animals.

➤ Sulfonamides act as competitive inhibitors for the incorporation of PABA to form Dihydropteroic acid.

➤ Trimethoprim is an inhibitor of dihydrofolate reductase required for the conversion of dihydrofolic acid in to tetrahydrofolic acid in bacteria.

Mechanism of resistance: - It may be due to

1. Increased production of PABA by resistant bacteria

2. Decrease the affinity of folate synthetase enzyme for sulfonamides.

3. Adopts an alternative pathway in folate metabolism. E.g.:- gonococci, pneumococci, E.coli, S.aureus etc

Cotrimoxazole: - fixed dose combination of trimethoprim and sulfamethoxazole in a ratio of (1:5). As this inhibits 2 different steps in pathway, the development of resistance is reduced.

Adverse reactions:-

1. Stevens Johnson's syndrome

2. Hemolytic anemia

3. Kernicterus (neonatal Hyperbilirubinemia)

4. Skinrash, Urticaria

5. Crystalluria is due to crystals of sulfanilamide, This can be presented by

    i)   Alkalanizing the urine

    ii)   By increasing the urine flow

    iii)   By reducing PKa of drug.

Metabolism: - It occurs by acetylation at N4 they are excreted as mixtures of unmetabolised drugs, N4 acetates & glucouronides. Sulfones: - less active than sulfonamides

M.O.A:- similar to sulfonamides. E.g.:- Dapsone

QUINOLONES

E.g.:- Nalidixic acid

Fluoroquinolones: - These are more potent than quinolones.

First generation: Norfloxacin, Ofloxacin, Ciprofloxacin, Perfloxacin.

Second generation: Sparfloxacin, Lomefloxacin.

M.O.A:- They inhibit Bacterial DNA gyrase (An enzyme responsible for introducing negative supercoiling in to circular duplex DNA.) Negative super coiling relieves the tortional stress of unwinding helical DNA & thereby allows transcription & replication to occur. Humans have Topoisamerase II in place of gyrase & this accounts for the low toxicity of FQ's to the host cells.

Resistance: - Due to chromosomal mutation producing a DNA gyrase with reduced affinity for FQ's. AR: - Hypersensitivity reactions, Hemolytic anemia GI disturbances.

Uses: - Typhoid, soft tissue infection, UTI.

B Lactam Antibiotics

E.g.:- Pencillins & Cephalosporins

M.O.A:- microorganism synthesize two pentapeptides –

1. UDP-N-acetyl muramic acid (NAMA)

2. UDP-N-acetyl glucosamine (NAGA)

These peptidoglycon residues are linked together in forming long strands & the UDP is split off. The final step is cleavage of the terminal D- Alanine by 'transpeptidase'. The energy released is utilized for establishment of crosslinkages between peptide chains of the neighbouring strands.

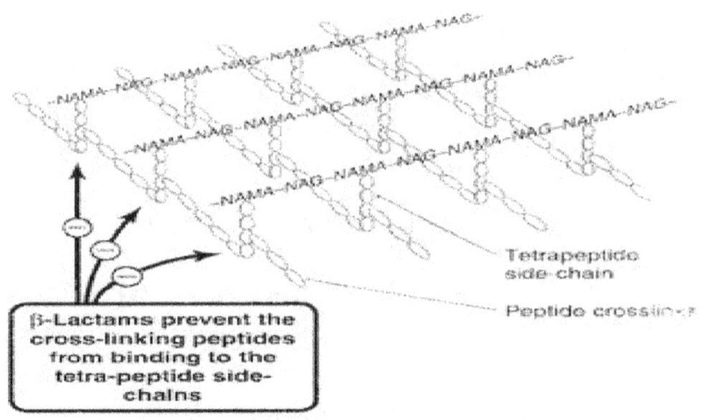

Beta lactam Antibiotics inhibit the enzyme 'transpeptidase' so that crosslinking does not take place. These enzymes constitute the pencillin binding proteins which are located in the bacterial cell membrane. When Bacteria divide in presence of a B-lactam antibiotic cell wall deficient forms are produced & these forms burst resulting in cell lysis.

Blood, pus & tissues fluids do not interfere with the antibacterial action of B-lactam Antibiotics.

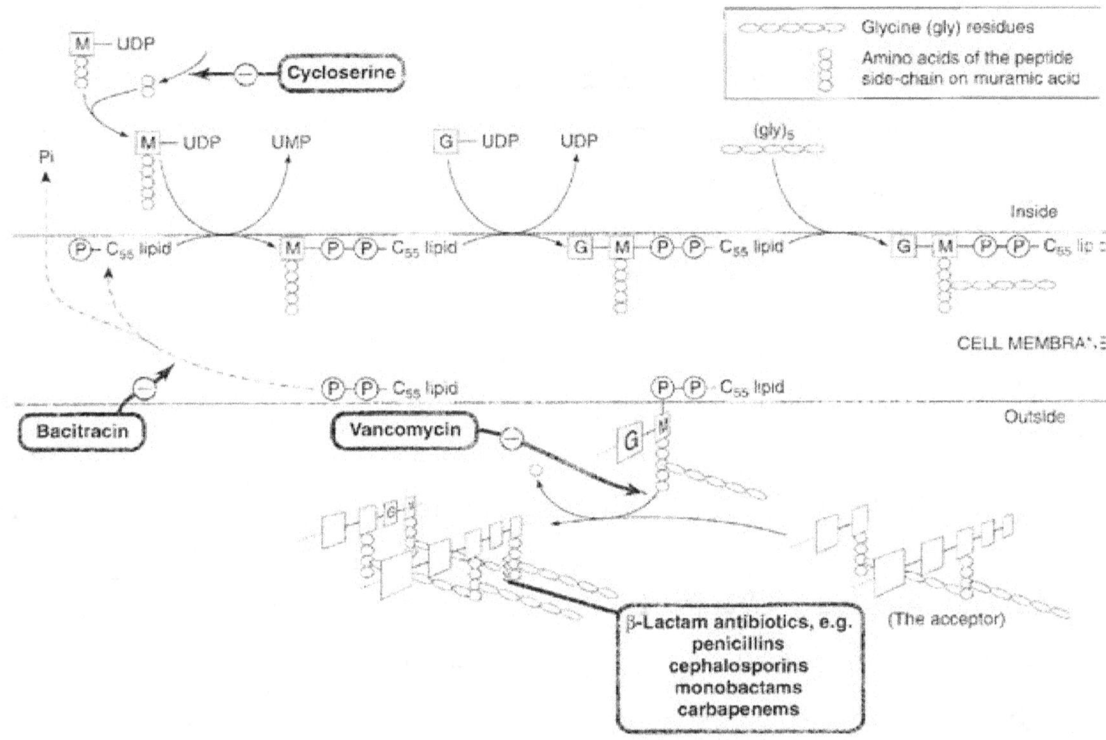

<u>**CLASSIFICATION OF PENICILLIN'S:-**</u>

☐ Natural: - Penicillin-G, procaine penicillinG

☐ Acid resistant: - Penicillin V (phenoxymethyl penicillin)

☐ Broad spectrum: - Ampicillin, Amoxicillin, Piperacillin Methicillin

☐ B lactamase inhibitors: - clavulonic acid, sulbactam

☐ Monobactams: - Aztreonam

☐ Carbapenems: - Imipenam, Thienamycin

<u>**BACTERIAL RESISTANCE: -**</u>

Gram positive organisms develop resistance by producing B-lactamases. (Opens B lactam ring & inactivates) In methicillin resistant S.aureus the penicillin Binding proteins has been mutated. So that it does not binds methicillin efficiently.

<u>AR</u>: - penicillin allergy due to formation of Antigenic penicilloyl proteins. Jarisch-Herxhemier reaction is Syphilis patient.

Degradation of penicillin can be controlled by adjusting the PH of aq-solutions between 6.0 – 6.8.

<u>USES</u>: -

Gonorrhea, Syphilis, Diphtheria & coccal infections. Augmentin = Clavulanic acid + Amoxicillin

Unasyn = Sulbactam + Ampicillin

<u>CLASSIFICATION OF CEPHALASPORINS</u>:-

Cephalosporin = B lactam ring + dihydrothiazine ring Penicillin = B lactam ring + thiazolidine ring.

	I	II	III	IV
Oral	Cephalexin	Axetal Cefaclor Cefuroxime	Cefixime Cefpodoxime	---
Parentral	Cephadroxil	Cefomandole Cefonacid	Cefotoxime Ceftriaxone	Cefepime

<u>Antipseudomonal Cephalosporins</u>: -

Cefoperazone, Moxalactam, Cefotaxime, Ceftizoxime & Ceftriaxone.

<u>Disulfiram effect</u>: -

Cefomandole, cefoperazone, cefometazone, cefotetan & moxolactam due to tetrazole group produce Disulfiram effect when taken with alcohol. Aztreonam is used to treat hospital acquired infections (Nosocomical infections).

<u>Tetracyclines, Chloramphenicol, Aminoglycoside and Macrolide antibiotics</u>

In order to understand the mechanism of the above antibiotics it is essential to understand the process of protein synthesis:

➢ On a specific signal from the cytoplasm, the DNA in the nucleus unwinds itself with the help of the enzyme DNA gyrate or topoisomerase (humans).

➢ One of the strands of the DNA acts a template for the synthesis of a complimentary strand of mRNA in the presence of RNA polymerase. The synthesis of mRNA from DNA is called transcription.

➢ The mRNA which now contains the code for protein synthesis comes out of the nucleus and attaches itself to the 30's ribosomal subunit.

➢ This is followed by the attachment of the 50's ribosomal subunit to the mRNA-ribosomal complex.

➢ There are two sites present on the 50's ribosomal subunit, the acceptor site and the peptidyl site.

➢ Protein synthesis does not begin until the mRNA has the initiator codon AUG (codes for formylmethionine) on it.

➢ Once the mRNA exposes the initiator codon AUG, a specific tRNA carrying the amino acid formylmethionine will arrive at the acceptor site of 50's subunit.

➢ The tRNA carrying the amino acid is now transferred to the peptidyl site where the tRNA dissociates leaving the amino acid at the peptidyl site.

➢ The ribosome now moves along the mRNA to expose the next coon.

➢ Depending upon the codon the corresponding amino acid is brought to the acceptor site by a specific tRNA.

➢ The tRNA carrying the amino acid is now transferred to the peptidyl site where the tRNA dissociates leaving the amino acid at the peptidyl site.

➢ Again, Ribosome now moves along the mRNA to expose next codon and this process continues until the mRNA shows one of the terminatory codons UAA or UAG or UGA. These terminatory codons are called non-sense codons, as they do not code for any particular amino acid.

➢ The transfer of data contained in the mRNA to form proteins is called translation.

➢ When only one ribosome is attached to the mRNA it is called monosome when there are more than one ribosome attached to the mRNA it is called polysome.

Antibiotic	Tetracycline	Chloramphenicol	Aminoglycoside	Macrolide
Source	Soil actinomycetes S.aureofaciens	Streptomyces Venezuelae	Streptomycin- S.griseus	Erythromycin- S.erythreus
Spectrum of Activity	Broad spectrum	Broad Spectrum	Active only against aerobes. Bactericidal	Active against mainly gram + organisms.
Mechanism of action	Binds to the 30's ribosomal subunit and inhibits the attachment of aminoacid-tRNA complex to the mRNA- ribosomal complex.	It acts by interfering with the transfer of the elongating peptide chain to the newly attached amino acid at the ribosome mRNA complex. Therefore, it inhibits peptide bond formation. It specifically attaches to 50's ribosome.	It binds to the 30's subunit, the 50's subunit as well to the 30s-50s interface. They freeze initiation of protein synthesis, prevent polysome formation. Binding to the 30s-50s interface causes distortion of the mRNA codon resulting in wrong amino acids entering the peptide chain and these defective proteins affect the integrity of the cell membrane resulting in cell death.	It combines with 50s ribosomal subunit and interferes with translocation of the elongated peptide chain back to the peptidyl site. The ribosome fails to move along the mRNA to expose the next codon and thus protein synthesis is terminated prematurely.
Mechanism of Resistance	Due to plasma mediated synthesis of a protection protein that protects the ribosomal binding site from TC's. Posess cross resistance with chloramphenicol.	Resistant organisms produce Chloramphenicol acetyl transferase, which inactivates the drug.	. Inactivating enzymes that adenylate/acetylate or phosphorylate the antibiotic. Decrease in the affinity of the ribosomal protein that binds the antibiotic. C. Porins become less permeable to the drug.	Resistant organisms produce erythromycin esterase that inactivates the drug or the organisms become less permeable to the drug.

Pharmacokin etics	TC's have chelating property- form insoluble and unabsorbable complexes with calcium and other metals.	Oral form is Chloramphenicol palmitate. Parenteral form is Chloramphenicol Succinate.	All ionize in solution and are not absorbed orally. Excreted unchanged in urine.	Erythromycin is acid labile. To protect it from the gastric acid it is given an enteric coat.
Adverse Effects Fanchony syndrome.	1. Liver damage 2. Kidney damage 3. Photo toxicity 4. Deposition of	a. Gray baby syndrome: seen in infants because they lack the glucoronic acid required for conjugation with	a. Ototoxicity ☐ Cochlear damage ☐ Vestibular damage b. Nephrotoxicity	Gastrointestinal distress a. Hepatitis.
Shown by only doxycycline	calcium tetracycline chelate in bones and teeth. Vestibular toxicity- Ataxia, vertigo and nystagmus (involuntary eye ball moment). Diabetes insipidus- Demeclocyclin	Chloramphenicol. b. Super infections Bonemarrow depression- aplasticanemia, agranulocytosis, thrombocytopenia.	c. Neuromuscular blockade	
Uses	a. Used to treat infections, when the causative organism is unknown. b. venereal diseases c. Cholera, plague, Brucellosis, etc.	a. Typhoid (enteric fever) b. H.influenzae meningitis c. Anaerobic infections D.Intraocular infections.	a. Tuberculosis b. SABE c. Plague d. Tularemia sub acute Bacterial endocarditis (sabe)	a. Atypical pneumonia caused by mycoplasma pneumoniae b. Diphtheria, tetanus, Syphilis, etc...

Tetracyclines:-

More stable & long acting -----------6-deoxy tetracycline, methacycline, doxycline minocycline.

<u>**Miscellaneous Antibiotics:-**</u>

1) <u>**Lincosamide antibiotics:**</u> - clindamycin M.O.A & spectrum of activity is similar to erythromycin & also exhibits partial cross resistance.

2) <u>**Glycopeptide Antibiotics:**</u> - E.g.:- Vancomycin acts by inhibiting cell wall synthesis. It binds to the terminal dipeptide sequence of peptidoglycon units at the cell membrane & their cross linking to form the cell wall does not take place.

<u>Uses</u>: - In MRSA infections.

3. <u>**Polypeptide Antibiotics:**</u> - Bactericidal agents have detergent like action on cell membrane. They have high affinity for phospholipids & thus they orient between phospholipid & the protein layers in gram negative organisms, resulting in formation of pseudopore. As a result aminoacids leak out leading to cell death. E.g.:- Polymyxin B, Bacitracin, Colistin, Thyrotricin, Capreomycin, Nespirocin.

<u>**Urinary Antiseptics:**</u> - Nitrofurantoin, Hexamine

<u>**Urinary Analgesic:**</u> - Phenazopyridine HCL.

<u>**ANTITUBERCULAR AGENTS**</u>

Tuberculosis is caused by mycobacterium tuberculosis.

<u>First line drugs</u>: - INH, Rifampicin, Pyrazinamide, Ethambutol. <u>Second line drugs</u>: - Ciprofloxacin, Azithromycin.

DRUG	M.O.A	PHARMACOKINETICS	A.R
P-amino salicylic acid	Prevents incorporation of PABA	It undergoes Acetylation At lowPH- decarboxylation At highPH-oxidation	Hypersensitivity reactions
I N H	Inhibits the synthesis of mycolic acid (imp component of mycobacterial cell wall)	Acetylated by liver.	Peripheral neuritis due to renal excretion of vit B_6 ,Hepatitis

Drug	M.O.A	Pharmacokinetics	A.R
Rifampicin	Inhibits DNA dependent RNA polymerase	Metabolized in liver to an active deacteylated metabolite.	Hepatitis respiratory syndrome, Cutaneous syndrome, Flu syndrome, Abdominal syndrome.
Pyrazinamide	Not known penetrates inflamed meninges in treatment of tuberculosis meningitis.	Penetrates CSF & metabolised in liver.	Hepatatoxicity, Hyperuricaemia (due to inhibition of uric acid tubular secretion)
Ethambutol (d isomer is more potent)	Interferes with mycolic acid incorporation in cell wall & inhibits RNA synthesis.	75% of oral dose is absorbed & temporarily stored in R.B.C.	Loss of visual acuity, field effects due to optic neuritis.

Antitubercular Antibiotics: - Cycloserine, Capreomycin, Viomycin, Rifampicin.

Effective treatment :- (Sterilization period).

INH 300mg, Rifampicin 600mg, Pyrazinamide 25mg/kg (for 8 weeks) (Maintainance period) INH & Rifampicin (for 16 weeks)

ANTILEPROTIC AGENTS

Leprosy is caused by *Mycobacterium leprae.*

Drug	M.O.A	Pharmacokinetics	A.R
Dapsone	Inhibits incorporation of PABA in to folic acid	Completely absorbed orally, gets concentrated in skin, liver & kidney.	Mild Hemolytic anemia, gastric intolerance.
Cycloserine	Inhibits bacterial cell wall synthesis by inhibiting the enzyme that racemises h-alanine and links two D- Alanine residues.		
Clofazimine (dye)	Binds with nucleic acids & concentrate in reticuloendothelial tissue & interfere with template function of DNA.	Gets accumulated in tissues especially in crystalline form.	Well tolerated reddish Block discolouration of skin

ANTIFUNGAL AGENTS

Classification:-

1. **Azoles: -** Clotrimazole, Ketaconazole, Miconazole.

2. **Allylamine & related compounds: -** Tolnafate, Terbinafine.

3. **Fatty acids: -** Propionic acid, Triacetin, Salicylic acid.

4. **Phenol & their derivatives: -** Haloprogin, Cyclopirox.

5. **Nucleosides: -** Flucytosine.

6. **Antibiotics: -** Nystatin, Amphotericin, Candidicin.

7. **Heterocyclic Benzofuran: -** Griseofulvum.

Drug	Amphotericin B	Griseofulvin	Imidazoles & triazoles.	Flucytosine	Tolnafate
Mechanism of action	Has high affinity for ergosterol present in fungal cell membrane. Binds to it forming a micropore, through which amino acids leak out leading to cell death.	It interferes with mitosis and causes abnormal metaphase configurations. The daughter nuclei fail to move apart and thus cell division is arrested at metaphase.	They inhibit the fungal cytochrome P_{450} enzyme lanosterol 14-demethylase required for conversion of lanosterol to ergosterol. This results in membrane abnormalities in the fungus.	It is taken up by fungal cells and then converted into 5-FU and then to 5-fluorodeoxyuridylic acid which is an inhibitor of thymidylate synthetase required for the synthesis of thymidylic acid, which is a component of DNA.	Interfere with fungal ergosterol Biosynthesis by epoxidation of squalene by the enzyme squalene epoxidase.
Spectrum of activity	Candida albicans, Histoplasma capsulatum, etc.	Dermatophytes such as Epidermophyton, Trichophyton, microsporum, etc.	Dermatophytes, candida albicans, nocardia, leishmania, etc.	Cryptococcus neoformans, chromoblastomyces.	Dermatophytes candida.

Pharmacoki netics	Administered both orally and prarenterally.	Gets deposited in the Keratin forming cells of skin, hair and nails. Absorption is enhanced by micronisation.		Administered orally	
Adverse effects	Nephrotoxicity-azotemia, g.f.r acidosis.	Peripheral neuritis, transient leukopenia, albuminuria.	Inhibits CYP3A4, thereby raising the blood levels of drugs like warfarin, terfenadine.	Leucopenia, thrombocytopenia.	
Uses	Systemic mycoses and Leishmaniasis.	Dermatophytosis.	Systematic and topical infections.	Chromoblastomycosis.	Athlete's foot ringworm.

Antiviral agents: Infectious virus particle is called virion.

DNA containing virus

Adenovirus	Many types	Respiratory tract & eye infections
Herpes virus	H.simplex I & II vercilla zoster Herpes zoster	Encephalitis chicken pox shingles
Papora virus	Human wart virus polyoma virus	Human wart salivary gland infection
Pox virus	Vaccine	Small pox, chicken pox, cow pox, eczema.

RNA CONTAINING VIRUS:-

Orthomyxovirus	Influenza A,B,D	Influenza A,B,D
Picornovirus	Rhinovirus	Respiratory disease poliomyletis
Retrovirus	Type C Type B Type D HIV	Leukemia Mammary tumor Monkey Aids AIDS
Rhabdovirus	Rabies virus	Rabies
Togavirus	Rubella virus	Rubella
Unclassified virus	Hepatitis A,B,&C viruses	Hepatitis

CLASSIFICATION:-

A. Anti-herpes virus. Most of the antiviral drugs of this class act by inhibiting DNA polymerase. E.g.:- Idoxuridine, acyclovir, Ganciclovir, Foscarnet.

B. Anti-retro virus. Non-nucleoside reverse transcriptase inhibitors. E.g.:- Zidovudine (AZT), Didanosine, and Zalcitabine. Nevirapine, Delaviridine. Protease inhibitors. E.g.:- Saquinavir, Indinavir.

C. Anti-influenza virus. E.g.:- amantadine.

D. Others. E.g.:- interferons, ribavirin.

Drug	Mechanism of action	Mechanism of resistance	Adverse effects	Uses
Idoxuridine	It is phosphorylated by viral thymidylate kinase to monophosphate, then to triphosphate. The triphosphate is an inhibitor of viral DNA polymerase, causing inhibition of viral DNA synthesis and it is also incorporated in the DNA resulting in faulty DNA, which code for wrong proteins.	Resistant viruses decrease the amount of thymidylate kinase required for the activation of the drug. Decrease in the affinity of DNA polymerase for the drug.		1. H.simplex keratoconjuctivities. (Cytomegalblasto virus)
Foscarnet	A phosphonoformate derivative binds to the pyrophosphate binding sites of viral DNA polymerase and reverse transcriptase to prevent the incorporation of nucleotides into DNA.		Hypokalemia, hypomagnesia, renal toxicity.	CMV retinitis, varicella zoster infections.
Zidovudine, Stavudine	On phosphorylation in the body into zidovudine triphosphate, it inhibits the enzyme viral reverse transcriptase which is required for the synthesis of DNA from viral RNA.	Decrease in the affinity of reverse transcriptase for the drug.	Anaemia, neutropenia, myopathy.	AIDS
Saquinavir	An aspartic enzyme protease encoded by HIV is involved in the production of structural protein and enzymes of the virus. Inhibition of the aspartic enzyme by Saquinavir will deprive the virus of the essential proteins.		G.i.t intolerance, asthenia, paresthesia and exacerbation of diabetes.	Used to treat later stages of AIDS infections.
Amantadine	It acts on an ion channel M2 and interferes with the step of uncoating.		Insomnia, dizziness, hallucination.	influenzaA2, Parkinson's.
Ribavirn	Its mono and triphosphate derivatives inhibit GTP and viral RNA synthesis.			InfluenzaA & B, measles.
Acylclovir	Converted to monophosphate by viral thymidine kinase.			Herpes infections.

Interferons: - are the cytokines produced by the body in response to viral infections. They bind to cell specific receptors and interfere with various stages of viral replication such as uncoating, penetration of virus into the host cell, synthesis of viral protein. Interferon's bind to receptors and induce production of Interferon induced protein that has antiviral effects. They are active against both DNA & RNA viruses. They are host specific. They are indicated for:-

- Chronic hepatitis B & C
- AIDS related Kaposi sarcoma (cancer & aids)
- Hairy cell leukemia.
- Rhinoviral cold.

Adverse effects include myelosupression, neurotoxicity, etc.

ANTIMALARIAL AGENTS

DRUG	CHLOROQUINE	MEFLOQUINE	QUININE	CHLOROGUANIDE PROGUANIL
Mechanism of action	It moves into acidic vesicles of the parasite, raises pH and inhibits the degradation of Hemoglobin by lysosomal products. It inhibits the enzyme haempolymerase nontoxic haemzoin.	Inhibits the enzyme haem polymerase.	Inhibits the enzyme haempolymerase.	It is cyclised in the body to a triazine derivative, which inhibits plasmodial dihydrofolate reductase, which is essential for the synthesis of folate coenzymes.
Resistance	It occurs due to the increased efflux of the drug from the parasitic vesicles.	Increased expression of an efflux transporter similar to human transporter, glycoprotein.	Increased expression of an efflux transporter similar to human transporter, P- glycoprotein.	It occurs by mutation resulting in decrease in the affinity of the DHFRase for drug.
Spectrum of activity	Erythrocytic stages of all the four plasmodial species.	Blood Schizonticide Against P.Falciparum & P.vivax.	Blood schizonticide on all the four plasmodial species.	Slow acting Schizonticide. Erythrocytic
Adverse effects	Liver damage.	Gastrointestinal disturbance,giddiness, insomnia.Prolongation of QT intervals leading to arrhythmias.	Cinchonism- tinnitus, paraplegia,	Mild abdominal upset, hematuria.
Uses	Also active	Treatment of an acute attack.	Resistant falciparum malaria, cerebral malaria.	Prophlaxis of malaria.

Malaria is caused by four species namely

1. plasmodium vivax,

2. P.falciparum,

3. P.malariae and P.ovale.

4. P.falciparum does not have secondary Schizontic stage.

CLASSIFICATION:-

1. Cinchona Alkaloids: - Quinine

2. 4 Amino quinoline: - Chloroquine, Amodiaquine

3. 8 Amino quinoline: - Primaquine, pamaquine

4. 9 Amino Acridines: - Quinacrine

5. Biguanides & dihydrotriazines: - Chlorguanide

6. Pyrimidines: - Pyrimethamine

7. Sulfonamides: - Sulfadoxine, Dapsone, Sulfamethopyrazine

8. Quinoline methanol: - Mefloquine

9. Phenanthrene methanol: - Halofantrine

10. Miscellaneous: - Qinghaosu, tetracycline's.

➤ Pyrimethamine also acts by inhibiting plasmodial dihydrofolate reductase and it is a more potent than chlorguanide.

➤ Primaquine acts on the exoerythrocytic stages and is highly active against the gametocytes and hypnozoites.

➤ It causes hemolytic anemia in patients with G6-PD deficiency.

➤ Halofantrine, a blood schizonticidal agent is active against multiresistant.

➤ P.falciparum. Cross-resistance is seen between Halofantrine and mefloquine.

➤ Artemesinin, a sesquiterpine lactone is active against multiresistant.

➤ P.falciparum. It acts by interacting with haem and generated free radicals that binds to the membrane proteins and damages the parasite.

ANTIAMOEBIC DRUGS

Ameobiasis is a protozoal disease caused by Entamoeba Histolytica.

Intestinal amoebiasis: - Here E.Histolytica invade the intestinal wall of the colon. **Extra intestinal amoebiasis:** - It affects liver, lungs & Brain.

E.Histolytica exists in two forms

1. Cysts: - inactive form

2. Trophozite: - active form

CLASSIFICATION:-

A. Tissue amoebicides

☐ For both intestinal and extra intestinal amoebiasis. Nitroimidazoles. E.g.: Metronidazole, tinidozole rhimostrozole. Alkaloids. E.g. : emetine

☐ For extra intestinal amoebiasis only. E.g. : chloroquine

B. Luminal amoebicides

☐ Amide. E.g. : Diloxanide furoate

☐ 8-Hydroxyquinolines. E.g.: Quiniodochlor, Diiodohydroxyquin clioquinol.

☐ Antibiotics. E.g.: Tetracycline's.

Drug	Metronidazole, tinidozole	Emetine	Diloxanide furoate	Quiniodochlor, Diiodohydroxyquin
Mechanism of action	The nitro group of the compound is reduced to intermediate compounds that cause cytotoxicity by damaging DNA.	It inhibits protein by arresting the intraribosomal translocation of peptidyl tRNA aminoacid complex.	It prevents the formation of cysts.	Kill the cyst forming trophozoites in the intestinal tract by chelating ferrous ions which are essential for protozoal metabolism.
Spectrum of activity	Anaerobic organisms.	Kills trophozoites but has no action on cysts.	Kills trophozoites responsible formation.	Active against entamoeba, Giardia trichomonas and some fungi.
Adverse effects	G.i.t disturbances, CNS symptoms.	Hypo tension, tachycardia, ECG myocarditis.	Flatulence, itchings occasional.	Iodism. Prolonged use caused 'sub acute myelopatic (SMON).
Uses	Amoebiasis, infections.	Liver fluke infestation	Asymptomatic amoebiasis.	Amoebiasis,Giardiasis, monolial vaginitis, fungal infections.

<u>**Suramin sodium:**</u> - anionic in nature & binds with cationic sites in proteins & enzymes in glycolytic pathway.

<u>**Sodium stilbogluconate:**</u> - These pentavalent antimonials get converted to trivalent antimonials, which inhibit phosphofructokinase, an enzyme catalyses a limiting step in glycolysis.

Leishmaniasis is caused by Leishmania donovani and the drugs used to

<u>ANTHELMINTICS</u>

These agents destroy or eliminate parasitic worms (helmints) from GIT/body
tissues.

Anthelmintic may act as:-

1) Vermifuge :- expels worms by paralyzing them

2) Vermicide :- kill worms in the body

3) Some may also impair the egg production process in worms.

Drug	Mebendazole/Albendazole	Pyrantel pamoate	Piperazine	Diethyl carbamazine
Mechanism of action	Inhibit glucose uptake, thereby depleting glycogen stores. Bind with affinity to micro tubular protein B-tubulin and inhibit its polymerization.	It causes activation of nicotinic cholinergic receptors in the worm resulting in persistent depolarization, which leads to paralysis. Worms are then expelled.	It causes neuromuscular blockade by antagonizing Ach action and causes hyperpolarisation, which leads to paralysis. Worms are then expelled.	Alteration of the Microfilariae (MF) membrane so that they are readily phagocytosed by tissue fixed monocytes.
Spectrum of activity	Round worm, hook worm, tirichuriasis, pinworm & guinea worm.	Hook worm Round worm, thread worm.	Round worm,	Mf of Wuchereria bancrofti, Brugia malayi, o.volvulus.

Drug	Levamisole	Niclosamide	Praziquantel	Ivermectin
Mechanism of action	It is an immunomodulator-restores T-cell function	It inhibits oxidative phosphorylationin mitochondria and thereby interferes with anaerobic generation of ATP.	Causes leakage of intracellular calcium from the membranes leading to paralysis. The lose grip of the intestine and are expelled.	Potentiation of GABAergic transmission in worms leading to paralysis.
Spectrum of activity	Ascaris & stronglyloides larvae.	Taenia saginata, T. solium, hymenlepsis nana.	Tape worms schistosomiasis.	Onchocerca volvulus, which causes river blindness.

ANTICANCER AGENTS

These are cytotoxic drugs either kill cancer cells or modify their growth cell cycle:

G_1 (pre-synthetic phase)

☐

S – Synthesis of DNA

☐

G_2 – Post synthetic phase

☐

M - Mitosis phase

☐ ☐

G_1 G_1 (daughter cells)

☐

G_0 – Resting phase

➢ The cells in resting stage are those that are non-proliferating.

➢ These remain quiescent, but they can be recruited in the cell cycle when stimulated later.

➢ Cytotoxic drugs are either cell cycle specific or cell cycle non-specific (they kill both resting as well as dividing cells).

o Cytotoxic drugs that are cell cycle specific include drugs like Methotrexate, Cytarabine, 6-Mercaptopurine, 6-Thioguanine, Mitomycin, Doxorubicin act on the S phase, drugs like Daunorubicin, Bleomycin, etoposide that act on the G_2, drugs like vincristine, Vinblastine and paclitaxel that act on the M phase.

o Cytotoxic drugs that are cell cycle nonspecific include nitrogen mustards, cyclophosphomide, Chlorambucil, 5-FU, L-asparginine, Cisplatin, Procarbazine, Dacarbazine, etc.

 CLASSIFICATION:

A. <u>Alkylating agents:</u> These can be further classified into:

a. Nitrogen mustards. E.g.: Mustine, Cyclophosphamide, Ifosfamide, chlorambucil

b. Ethyleneimine. E.g.: Thiotepa

c. Alkylsulfonate. E.g.: Busulphan

d. Nitrosourea. E.g.: Carmustine, Lomustine (they cross B.B.B & used in Brain tumors)

e. Triazine. E.g.: Dacarbazine.

f. Hydrazine. E.g.: Procarbazine

B. Antimetabolites

a. Folate antagonist. E.g.: Methotrexate (amethopterin)

b. Purine antagonist. E.g.: 6-Mercaptopurine, Azathiopurine, 6-Thioguanine

c. Pyrimidine antagonist. E.g.: 5-Fluorouracil, Cytarabine.

C. Vinca alkaloids. E.g.: Vincristine (oncovin), Vinblastine.

D. Taxanes. E.g.: paclitaxel, Taxotere.

E. Epipodophyllotoxin. E.g.: etoposide, Teniposide Daunorubicin.

F. Antibiotics. E.g.: Actinomycin D (Dactinomycin), Doxorubicin Bleomycins, Mitomycin.

G. Miscellaneous. E.g.: cisplatin, L-asparaginase.

TOXICITY OF ANTICANCER DRUGS:-

They have a profound effect on rapidly proliferating cells, the most important target of action are the nucleic acids and their precursors; rapid nucleic acid synthesis occurs during cell division. The different Toxicities that arise from Anticancer agents are:-

1. Bone marrow depression (Myelo suppression / Blood dyscriasis) resulting in granulocytopenia, agranulocytosis, thrombocytopenia, Aplastic anemia

2. Lymphocytopenia and the suppression of Humoral & Cell mediated immunity.

3. Stomatitis, diaarohea, shedding of mucosa, hemmorages

4. Skin: Alopecia

5. Inhibition of gonadal cells causes oligozoospermia& impotence in males.

6. Teratogenic in nature.

7. Hyperuricaemia

Virus: - Epstein barr virus is responsible for production of cancer Genes: -

Oncogene is responsible for production of cancer

ALKYLATING AGENTS: -

☐ These compounds produce highly reactive carbonium intermediates, which transfer alkyl groups to cellular macromolecules by forming covalent bonds. The position 7 of guanine residues in DNA is highly susceptible because it is highly nucleophilic.

☐ This results in cross linking / abnormal base pairing / scission of DNA strand.

☐ Crosslinking of nucleic acids can also take place.

☐ In case of Meclorethamine (mustine), Aziridinium is the intermediate formed.

☐ In case of Cyclophosphamide, Phosphoramide & Acrolein are the intermediates formed.

☐ **Phosphoramide is the active metabolite; While Acrolein is toxic to the Urinary bladder.**

☐ (Mercapto sulphonic acid is given to avoid damage of urinary bladder due to Acrolein)

☐ Ifosfamide is the congener of Cyclophosphamide.

☐ Thiotepa produces Aziridinium as an intermediate.

☐ Alkyl sulfonates undergo a process known as "Sulphur Stripping" to react with cellular macromolecules & is used in Myeloid Leukemia.

☐ Carmustine & Lomustine crosses B.B.B. and hence used in treatment of Brain Tumors

ANTIMETABOLITES: - These compounds prevent biosynthesis or utilization of normal cellular macromolecules.

FOLATE ANTAGONISTS: -

☐ Methotrexate (Amethopterine) / Aminopterine act by inhibiting dihydrofolate reductase (DHFR), which is essential for the conversion of Dihydrofolic acid to Tetrahydrofolic acid, & step which has to occur if synthesis of folate co-enzymes has to proceed.

☐ Thus, they inhibit the synthesis of thymidilic acid, which is a component of the DNA.

☐ Administration of Folinic acid counteracts toxicity of Methotrexate.

☐ Methotrexate acts on S phase of the cell division.

PURINE ANTAGONISTS: -

☐ 6-mercaptopurine, 6-thioguanine are converted to monoribonucleotide by Hypoxanthine guanine phosphoribosyl transferase (HGPRT).

☐ Tumor cells lack the enzyme HGPRT develop resistance to the above drugs.Monoribonucleotides inhibit the conversion of 5-Phosphoribosylpyrophosphate to 5-phosphoribosylamine, which is required for the synthesis of purines.

PYRIMIDINE ANTAGONISTS: -

➢ **5-fluorouracil is converted in the body to the corresponding nucleotide.**

➢ **5-**fluro-2-deoxyuridine monophosphate, which inhibits thymidilate synthetase & blocks the conversion of deoxyuridilic acid to deoxy thymidilic acid. Thus, it inhibits the synthesis of DNA.

➢ Fluorouracil itself gets incorporated in to nucleic acids and this may contribute to its toxicity.

Cytarabine: -

➢ It is phosphorylated in the body to the corresponding nucleotide, which inhibits DNA synthesis.

➢ The triphosphate of cytarabine is an inhibitor of DNA polymerase & blocks the generation of cytidilic acid.

Vinca alkaloids: -

➢ These are mitotic inhibitors that bind to the micro tubular protein "tubulin", prevent its polymerization & assembly of microtubules & thus cause disruption of mitotic spindle &interfere with cytoskeletal function.

➢ Therefore the chromosomes fail to move apart during mitosis.

➢ They are cell cycle specific and they act in metaphase phase. E.g.: vincristine & vinblastine

Taxanes: -

- Paclitaxel enhances polymerization of tubulin. As a result, the microtubules are stabilized & their depolymerisation is prevented.
- This stability results IU inhibition of normal dynamic reorganization of the microtubule network that is essential for vital interphase & mitotic functions. Abnormal arrays or bundles of microtubules are produced throughout the cell cycle.
- The major adverse effects seen are "stocking & glove" neuropathy.

DRUG	MECHANISM OF ACTION
Actinomycin D (Dactinomycin)	It inhibits DNA topoisomerase-2 & also interrelates in DNA, causing DNA breaks
Daunorubicin(Rubidomycin),Doxorubicin	It inhibits DNA topoisomerase-2& generates quinone type free radicals.
Mitomycin	It is converted in the body to act as an alkylating agent.
Hydroxyurea	It blocks the conversion of ribonucleotides to deoxy ribonucleotides by inhibitingthe enzyme ribonucleoside diphosphate reductase & thus interferes with DNAsynthesis.
Procarbazine	After metabolic activation, it depolymerises DNA & causes chromosomal damage. Inhibition of DNA synthesis occurs.
L-asparginase	The enzyme L-Asparginase degrades l-asparginase to L-aspartic acid, depriving leukemic cells of an essential metabolite & this may cause cell death.
Cisplatin	A platinum co-ordination complex is hydrolysed intracellularly to produce a highly reactive moiety that causes cross-linking of DNA.

- Epipodophyllotoxins such as etoposide arrest cells in the G_2 Phase & causes DNA breaks by stimulating DNA topoisomerase-2.

<u>**DIAGNOSTIC TESTS OF DISEASES:-**</u>

Diseases	Test
1.Diptheria	Shick test
2.Haemophilus	Ducrey test
3.Leprosy	Lepromin test
4.Scarlet fever	Dick test
5.Syphilus	VDRL & Widal test
6.Tuberculosis	Tuberculin test
7.Typhoid	Widal test

Deficiency disorder	Drug given
Hypocalcaemia	Calcium gluconate i.v. Corticosteroid
2. Addisons disease	Ferrous sulphate
3.Anaemia	

Toxicity	Drugs
1.Paracetamol, Chloroform	Acetyl cysteine
2.Copper,Gold	Penicillamine
3.Arsenic	Dimercaprol
4.Lead	Calcium EDTA
5.Iron	Desferroxamine
6.Benzodiazepines	Flumenazil
CO, CO_2	Oxygen
Caffeine, Theophylline	Esmolol

ANTIBIOTICS & CHEMOTHERAPY PHARMACOLOGY

ANTIBIOTICS BY CLASS				
GENERIC NAME	**BRAND NAMES**	**COMMON USE**	**POSSIBLE SIDE EFFECT**	**MECHANISM OF ACTION**
AMINOGLYCOSIDES				
Amikacin	Amikin	Infections caused by Gram-negative bacteria, such as *Escherichia coli* and *Klebsiella* particularly *Pseudomonas aeruginosa*. Effective against Aerobic bacteria (not obligate/ facultative anaerobes) andtularemia.	Hearing loss Vertigo Kidney damage	Binding to the bacterial 30S ribosomal subuni t (some work by binding to the 50S subunit), inhibiting the translocation of the peptidyl- tRNA from the A-site to the P- site and also causing misreading of mRNA, leaving the bacterium unable to synthesize proteins vital to its growth.
Gentamicin	Garamycin			
Kanamycin	Kantrex			
Neomycin	Neo-Fradin			
Netilmicin	Netromycin			
Tobramycin	Nebcin			
Paromomycin	Humatin			
ANSAMYCINS				
Geldanamycin		Experimental, As antitumor antibiotics		
Herbimycin				
CARBACEPHEM				
Loracarbef	Lorabid	Discontinued		Prevents bacterial cell division by inhibiting cell wall synthesis.
CARBAPENEMS				
Ertapenem	Invanz	Bactericidal for both Gram-positive and Gram-negative organisms and therefore useful for empiric broad-spectrum antibacterial coverage. (Note MRSA resistance to this class.)	Gastrointestinal upset and diarrhea Nausea Seizures Headache, Rash and allergic reactions	Inhibition of cell wall synthesis
Doripenem	Doribax			
Imipenem Cilastatin	Primaxin			
Meropenem	Merrem			
CEPHALOSPORINS (FIRST GENERATION)				
Cefadroxil	Duricef	Good coverage against	Gastrointestinal upset and	Same mode of action as

Cefazolin	Ancef (discontinued)	Gram positive infections.	diarrhea Nausea (if alcohol taken concurrently) Allergic reactions	other beta-lactam antibiotics: disrupt the synthesis of thepeptidoglycan layer of bacterial cell walls.
Cefalotin or Cefal othin	Keflin (discontinued)			
Cefalexin	Keflex			
CEPHALOSPORINS (SECOND GENERATION)				
Cefaclor	Distaclor	Less gram positive cover, improved gram negative cover.	Gastrointestinal upset and diarrhea, Nausea (if alcohol taken concurrently) Allergic reactions	Same mode of action as other beta-lactam antibiotics: disrupt the synthesis of thepeptidoglycan layer of bacterial cell walls.
Cefamandole	Mandol (discontinued)			
Cefoxitin	Mefoxin (discontinued)			
Cefprozil	Cefzil			
Cefuroxime	Ceftin, Zinnat (UK)			
CEPHALOSPORINS (THIRD GENERATION)				
Cefixime	Suprax	Improved coverage of Gram negative organisms, except Pseudomonas. Reduced Gram positive cover.	Gastrointestinal upset and diarrhea Nausea (if alcohol taken concurrently) Allergic reactions	Same mode of action as other beta-lactam antibiotics: Disrupt the synthesis of thepeptidoglycan layer of bacterial cell walls.
Cefdinir	Omnicef, Cefdiel			
Cefditoren	Spectracef			
Cefoperazone	Cefobid (discontinued)			
Cefotaxime	Claforan			
Cefpodoxime	Vantin			
Ceftazidime	Fortaz			
Ceftibuten	Cedax			
Ceftizoxime	Cefizox (discontinued)			
Ceftriaxone	Rocephin			

CEPHALOSPORINS (FOURTH GENERATION)				
Cefepime	Maxipime	Covers pseudomonal infections.	Gastrointestinal upset and diarrhea Nausea (if alcohol taken concurrently) Allergic reactions	Same mode of action as other beta-lactam antibiotics: disrupt the synthesis of thepeptidoglycan layer of bacterial cell walls.
CEPHALOSPORINS (FIFTH GENERATION)				
Ceftaroline fosamil	Teflaro	Used to treat MRSA	Gastrointestinal upset and diarrhea Allergic reaction	Same mode of action as other beta-lactam antibiotics: Disrupt the synthesis of thepeptidoglycan layer of bacterial cell walls.
Ceftobiprole	Zeftera	Used to treat MRSA	Gastrointestinal upset and diarrhea Nausea (if alcohol taken concurrently) Allergic reactions	Same mode of action as other beta-lactam antibiotics: Disrupt the synthesis of thepeptidoglycan layer of bacterial cell walls.

GLYCOPEPTIDES				
Teicoplanin	Targocid (UK)	Active agaist aerobic and anaerobic Gram positive bacteria including MRSA; Vancomycin is used orally for the treatment of C. difficile		Inhibiting peptidoglycan synthesis
Vancomycin	Vancocin			
Telavancin	Vibativ			
LINCOSAMIDES				
Clindamycin	Cleocin	Serious staph-, pneumo-,	Possible C.	Bind to 50S subunit of

Lincomycin	Lincocin	and streptococcal infections in penicillin-allergic patients, also anaerobic infections; clindamycin topically for acne	diff icile- related pseudomembranous enterocolitis	bacterial ribosomal RNAthereby inhibiting protein synthesis
LIPOPEPTIDE				
Daptomycin	Cubicin	Gram-positive organisms		Bind to the membrane and cause rapid depolarization, resulting in a loss of membrane potential leading to inhibition of protein, DNA and RNA synthesis

MACROLIDES				
Azithromycin	Zithromax, Sumamed, Xithrone	Streptococcal infections, syphilis, upper respiratory tract infections, lower respiratory tract infections, mycoplasmal infections, Lyme disease	Nausea, vomiting diarrhea (especially at high doses) Prolonged QT interval (especially erythromycin) Jaundice	Inhibition of bacterial protein biosynthesis by binding reversibly to the subunit 50S of the bacterial ribosome, There by inhibiting translocation of peptidyl tRNA.
Clarithromycin	Biaxin			
Dirithromycin	Dynabac (discontinued)			
Erythromycin	Erythocin,Erythr oped			
Roxithromycin				
Troleandomycin	Tao (discontinued)			
Telithromycin	Ketek	Pneumonia	Visual Disturbance, Liver Toxicity.[4]	
Spectinomycin	Trobicin	Gonorrhea		
Spiramycin	Rovamycine	Mouth infections		
MONOBACTAMS				
Aztreonam	Azactam			Same mode of action as other beta- lactam antibiotics: Disrupt the synthesis of

				thepeptidoglycan layer of bacterial cell walls.
Nitrofurans				
Furazolidone	Furoxone	Bacterial or protozoal diarrhea orenteritis		
Nitrofurantoin	Macrodantin, Macrobid	Urinary tract infections		
PENICILLINS				
Amoxicillin	Novamox, Amoxil	Wide range of infections; penicillin used for streptococcal infections, syphilis, Lyme disease	Gastrointestinal upset and diarrhea Allergy with seriousanaphylactic reactions Brain and kidney damage (rare)	Same mode of action as other beta-lactam antibiotics: Disrupt the synthesis of thepeptidoglycan layer of bacterial cell walls.
Ampicillin	Principen (discontinued)			
Azlocillin				
Carbenicillin	Geocillin (discontinued)			
Cloxacillin	Tegopen (discontinued)			
Dicloxacillin	Dynapen (discontinued)			
Flucloxacillin	Floxapen(Sold to European			

		generics Actavis Group)		
Mezlocillin	Mezlin (discontinued)			
Methicillin	Staphcillin (discontinued)			
Nafcillin	Unipen (discontinued)			
Oxacillin	Prostaphlin (discontinued)			
Penicillin G	Pentids (discontinued)			
Penicillin V	Veetids (Pen-Vee-K) (discontinued)			
Piperacillin	Pipracil (discontinued)			
Penicillin G	Pfizerpen			
Temocillin	Negaban (UK) (discontinued)			

Ticarcillin	Ticar (discontinued)			
PENICILLIN COMBINATIONS				
Amoxicillin clavulanate	Augmentin			The second component prevents bacterialresistance to the first component
Ampicillin sulbactam	Unasyn			
Piperacillin tazobactam	Zosyn			
Ticarcillin clavulanate	Timentin			
POLYPEPTIDES				
Bacitracin		Eye, ear or bladder infections; usually applied directly to the eye or inhaled into the lungs; rarely given by injection, although the use of intravenous colistin is experiencing a resurgence due to the emergence of multi drug resistant organisms.	Kidney and nerve damage (when given by injection)	Inhibits isoprenyl pyrophosph ate, a molecule that carries the building blocks of the peptidoglycanbacterial cell wall outside of the inner membrane
Colistin	Coly-Mycin-S			Interact with the gram
Polymyxin B				negative bacterial outer membrane and cytoplasmic membrane. It displaces bacterial counter ions, which destabilizes the outer membrane. They act like a detergent against the cytoplasmic membrane, which alters its permeability. Polymyxin B and E are bactericidal even in an isosmotic solution.

QUINOLONES				
Ciprofloxacin	Cipro, Ciproxin, Ciprobay	Urinary tract infections, bacterial prostatitis, community-acquiredpneumonia, bacterial diarrhea, mycoplasmal infections, gonorrhea	Nausea (rare), irreversible damage to central nervous system(uncommon), tendinosis (rare)	Inhibit the bacterial DNA gyrase or thetopoisomerase IV enzyme, There by inhibiting DNA replication and transcription.
Enoxacin	Penetrex			
Gatifloxacin	Tequin			
Levofloxacin	Levaquin			
Lomefloxacin	Maxaquin			
Moxifloxacin	Avelox			
Nalidixic acid	NegGram			
Norfloxacin	Noroxin			
Ofloxacin	Floxin, Ocuflox			
Trovafloxacin	Trovan	Withdrawn		
Grepafloxacin	Raxar	Withdrawn		
Sparfloxacin	Zagam	Withdrawn		
Temafloxacin	Omniflox	Withdrawn		
SULFONAMIDES				
Mafenide	Sulfamylon	Urinary tract infections (except sulfacetamide, used for eye infections, and mafenide and silver sulfadiazine, used topically forburns)	Nausea, vomiting, and diarrhea Allergy(including skin rashes) Crystals in urine Kidney failure Decrease inwhite blood cellcount Sensitivity to sunlight	Folate synthesis inhibition. They are competitive inhibitors of the enzyme dihydropteroate synthetase, DHPS. DHPS catalyses the conversion of PABA (*para*-aminobenzoate) to dihydropteroate, a key step in folate synthesis. Folate is necessary for the cell to
Sulfonamidochrys Iodine (archaic)	Prontosil			
Sulfacetamide	Sulamyd, Bleph-10			
Sulfadiazine	Micro-Sulfon			
Silver sulfadiazine	Silvadene			
Sulfamethizole	Thiosulfil Forte			
Sulfamethoxazole	Gantanol			
Sulfanilimide (archaic)				
Sulfasalazine	Azulfidine			synthesize nucleic acids (nucleic acids
Sulfisoxazole	Gantrisin			

Trimethoprim-Sulfamethoxazole (Co-trimoxazole) (TMP-SMX)	Bactrim, Septra			are essential building blocks of DNA andRNA), and in its absence cells will be unable to divide.

TETRACYCLINES				
Demeclocycline	Declomycin			
Doxycycline	Vibramycin		Gastrointestinal upset Sensitivity to sunlight Potential toxicity to mother and fetus during pregnancy Enamel hypoplasia (staining of teeth; potentially permanent) transient depression of bone growth	Inhibiting the binding of aminoacyl-tRNA to them RNA-ribosome complex. They do so mainly by binding to the 30S ribosomal subunit in the mRNA translation complex.
Minocycline	Minocin	Syphilis, chlamydial infections, Lyme disease, Mycoplasmal infections, Acne rickettsialinfections, * malaria * Note: Malaria is caused by a protist and not a bacterium.		
Oxytetracycline	Terramycin			
Tetracycline	Sumycin, Achromycin V, Steclin			

DRUGS AGAINST MYCOBACTERIA				
Clofazimine	Lamprene	Antileprotic		
Dapsone	Avlosulfon	Antileprotic		

Capreomycin	Capastat	Antituberculosis		
Cycloserine	Seromycin	Antituberculosis, urinary tract infections		
Ethambutol	Myambutol	Antituberculosis		
Ethionamide	Trecator	Antituberculosis		Inhibits peptide synthesis
Isoniazid	I.N.H.	Antituberculosis		
Pyrazinamide	Aldinamide	Antituberculosis		
Rifampicin (Rifampin in US)	Rifadin, Rimactane	mostly Gram-positive andmycobacteria	Reddish-orange sweat, tears, and urine	Binds to the β subunit of RNA polymerase to inhibit transcription
Rifabutin	Mycobutin	Mycobacterium avium complex	rash, discolored urine, GI symptoms	
Rifapentine	Priftin	Antituberculosis		

Streptomycin		Antituberculosis	Neurotoxicity,ototoxicity	As other aminoglycosides
OTHERS				
Arsphenamine	Salvarsan	Spirochaetal infections (obsolete)		
Chloramphenicol	Chloromycetin	Meningitis, MRSA, topical use, or for low cost internal treatment. Historic: typhus, cholera. gram negative, gram positive, anaerobes	Rarely: aplastic anemia.	Inhibits bacterial protein synthesis by binding to the 50S subunit of the ribosome

Fosfomycin	Monurol	Acute cystitis in women		Inactivates enolpyruvyl transferase, thereby blocking cell wall synthesis
Fusidic acid	Fucidin			
Linezolid	Zyvox	VRSA	Thrombocytopenia	
Metronidazole	Flagyl	Infections caused by anaerobic bacteria; also amoebiasis, trichomoniasis, Giardiasis	Discolored urine, headache, metallic taste, nausea ; alcohol is contraindicated	Produces toxic free radicals which disrupt DNA and proteins. This non-specific mechanism is responsible for its activity against a variety of bacteria, Amoebae, and protozoa.
Mupirocin	Bactroban	Ointment for impetigo, cream for infected cuts		Inhibits isoleucine t-RNA synthetase (IleRS) causing inhibition of protein synthesis
Platensimycin				
Quinupristin/ Dalfopristin	Synercid			
Rifaximin	Xifaxan	Traveler's diarrhea caused by *E. coli*		

Thiamphenicol		Gram-negative, Gram-positive, anaerobes. Widely used in veterinary medicine.	Lacks known anemic side- effects.	A chloramphenicol analog. May inhibit bacterial protein synthesis by binding to the 50S subunit of the ribosome
Tigecycline	Tigacyl			
Tinidazole	Tindamax Fasigyn	protozoan infections	upset stomach, bitter taste, and itchiness	
Trimethoprim	Proloprim, Trimpex	Urinary Tract Infections